Repeat After Me

UNDERSTANDING the
POWER of OUR WORDS

CHESSA JOHNSTON

ISBN 978-1-64492-673-4 (paperback)
ISBN 978-1-64492-674-1 (digital)

Christian Faith Publishing, Inc.
832 Park Avenue
Meadville, PA 16335
www.christianfaithpublishing.com

Printed in the United States of America

This book is dedicated to my mom, Bonnie, who has been listening to my words longer than anyone. Thank you for teaching me to love God and His Word. I love you, Mom!

To my husband, Justin- Thank you for loving me, supporting every new idea and thing I have wanted to do, and most of all for our life together. Love you.

To my four amazing boys, Michael, Lucas, Caleb and Adam - You four are my greatest joy and the best gifts I have ever received. Each one of you are my "favorite" and I love you with all of my heart.

CHAPTER 1

Me, Myself and My Mouth

Ever since I could remember, I have always loved to talk. Apparently, before I could remember, I loved to talk. My mom loves telling the story about me having a conversation with the wall while I was sitting in my high chair at the age of two. I don't think there ever was a year in elementary school or high school where I wasn't either getting my name on the board or being called out by the teacher for talking. Asking me to "stop talking, so we can go home" after church is a normal Sunday activity for my children.

I don't even need other humans or walls (unbeknownst to my two-year-old self) to talk. I can have a wonderful, fulfilling, intelligent conversation with yours truly. I don't even know why my husband asks, "Are you talking to yourself again," anymore. Of course, I am talking to myself; who else would I be talking with alone in my room or in the bathroom? Umm, me. I have found out that I am, hands down, my best listener. I can have full-blown conversations with myself or, if I am feeling so inclined, a pretend person or group of people. I have even spoken to crowds. Scary, I know. (I'm pretty sure that confession just lost me a few friends and possibly a few readers.)

I love to talk. I love words. I love communicating, laughing, telling jokes, stories, teaching Bible study, or what I am learning at the time. Talking is fun. I talk so much that when I don't talk, people get concerned. When I choose to not use a lot of words, my husband looks at me funny and asks, "Are you okay? You're quiet." Sometimes, I just answer, "Yeah, why?" (confused as to why anyone would ask me this). My poor husband; he wants more quietness from me, I'm sure, but then when I am quiet, it scares him. He can't win.

In the last forty years of my life, I have learned *a lot* about myself in this area. For some of you, forty years means I am still a baby: still have more to learn (which I totally agree with). To the youngsters reading this, forty years is *old*. I should know everything by now; should have this life thing mastered—I am literally staring death in the face. In reality, I am halfway done with my life on this earth, but I am forever learning as are you. Twenty years from now, when I look back at this book, I am probably going to say, "Wow. I really didn't know anything."

I am writing this book not only to my readers but to myself. I am forever trying to control this mouth of mine. My mom admitted to me a few years back that she would invite me over when they knew they were having people for dinner that would be hard to have conversations with. I was flattered and offended at the same time. Thanks, Mom! Wait a second… As I write this, I suddenly am thinking about how I could make this into a side-hustle and make some money.

"Having someone over who is hard to talk to? Don't worry! We have it covered! Just invite Gab Girl over, and the conversation will be endless! You'll never have to worry about awkward silence again!" I was a "filler" of sorts and had the "gift of gab." I could and still can talk about *anything* to *anyone*, and I mean it.

My words and talking have actually helped some people during my life, or so I'd like to think. People have said to me, "I will never forget when you said —— and it helped me so much", or "Remember when you used to say ——! It was so funny! "I actually don't know about that last one. I just like to think that I am funny even though my husband says I'm not. He's in denial.

I have given advice and wisdom to people that were walking through hard places that I had already tread on. I have spoken scripture over friends, family, and my children to encourage them and give them strength. In all of my many words, some of it has brought some good things to people. On the flip side, there have been many times that my words were less than helpful, selfish, angry, bitter, jealous, snarky, unnecessary, and just plain mean. You see, with many words come some words that hurt too.

I have said a lot of things that I am not proud of, ashamed of, and wish I could take back. I have spoken mean words to friends, my boys, my husband, my mom, siblings, in-laws, and strangers. I have also gossiped, slandered, and said horrible things behind other people's backs. I have told others things about myself that I shouldn't have and repeated sensitive information that was told to me in secrecy. I have lied, boasted, and exaggerated.

In the absence of talking, I have kept silent when I should have spoken up. The times I did not speak when I should have, ironically, are some of my biggest regrets. I am not an expert on your words or words in general for that matter, but *I am* an expert on my words because they are mine and I am the only one who gives myself permission to use them. I am not telling you all of this because I have it all figured out. I am writing this because it has always been an area that I have needed help in.

Our words can be used for great things but also for some of the most heinous and hurtful things. Our ability to communicate with our mouths is an amazing gift from God! Our voices can be powerful and beautiful or scary and destructive. One of the most incredible visuals that I have ever heard about words is this: "Words are like toothpaste: once they are out, they can't be put back in." Ouch. That's like a punch in the gut for me.

I always say my ability to talk is a blessing and a curse. It's the one thing that, as I get older, I have become so aware of. I want my words to be used for good, not harm. I want my words to matter, to uplift, give wisdom, and be helpful. Don't get me wrong, I am *not* mastering this; I repeat, *not* mastering. I have though become so much more cognizant of what is coming out of my mouth. Speaking the right words has become so important to me lately that I started reading verses in God's Word about the mouth and wisdom in speaking *every day*.

I am so serious about my words right now, it's not even funny. I even spouted off a verse from Proverbs the other day when my thirteen-year-old kept interrupting me while I was speaking to him. "You know, in the Bible it says, 'A person who answers before listening, that is his folly and shame.'" He just rolled his eyes and said, "Okay." I don't know if God addresses eye-rolling, but I will be definitely looking for it. I am all about parenting my children's weaknesses with scripture, apparently.

Our words matter, you guys. They are the crux of communication, learning, relationships, prayer, our careers, and worship. they have a lot of weight whether they're good or bad. They have consequences and power over our minds and actions. I cannot emphasize the importance of words. Heck, this book is full of them! That's what books are! Words, words, words! Unless it's a picture book. You get the gist, I hope.

Words are so important that those who cannot speak use sign language to get their "words" out. Friends, our words have *power*. Proverbs 18:21 says, "The tongue has the power of life and death…" To understand that we have the ability to bring life or death to something or someone because of what we say should be taken seriously. It should be humbling.

Most of the time in our culture today, words are just thrown out without thought. People just say whatever they feel like, so they can be heard or be popular to get attention. How many Facebook and Instagram posts have we put out there in frustration or arrogance only to cause an argument or misunderstanding all because we couldn't keep our words to ourselves? More than you or I would like to admit, I'm sure. Put the phone down, people. Your life will go on even if your extremely important opinion isn't on the internet, for the world to see.

We need to start looking at our words differently. We need to use them and disperse them with discernment. We need to be careful where and on whom they fall even to ourselves. If you get anything out of this book, I want it not to be that you would stress and worry so much about what you say that you don't even speak anymore or think so much about what you're going to say that it takes an eternity to hear your voice, but that you would be aware of what you say. Speak on purpose. Learn when to speak and when to, as I like to say, "hush your mouth". Are we thinking before we talk? Are we understanding the importance of our words? Are we counting the cost of the consequences?

To start off 2018, I decided to do something a little different instead of the traditional "New Year's Resolution" thing. I don't think I had *ever* kept a resolution. I liked the idea of having a goal and bettering myself. It felt good knowing what needed to be fixed and having an endgame: fix it. *But,* I never fixed any of those things despite my best intentions. I started to be negative about resolutions and stopped making them.

When January 2018 rolled around, I took a different approach to "change." I had read plenty of books and articles on building habits, changing the way I thought, making new "paths" in my brain, knowing that it took ninety days to completely build a new habit. Instead of just stating my resolution, doing great for about a month or so, then going back to my old self, I bought a notebook at the Dollar General and made a list.

I titled my notebook "2018 Spiritual Growth Goals." I then listed the things in my life that I knew I needed help with in my walk with God: to be more like Jesus. I put a few verses under each character trait or part of my life that I wanted to change and, in just a few sentences, described a few details of what that change looked like to me.

I committed to reading them along with the verses every day or at least every other day for all of 2018. I knew that if I read those verses and the things that I wanted to change, it would become a habit for me to think about them and a habit to want to change them. Do not ever minimize the effect of repetition. Even when it is boring, it is forming literal pathways into your brain; making it a habit and subconscious action. One of those growth goals was in the area of my mouth.

Oh, my mouth. It needs to be watched, guarded, and locked up sometimes. This is definitely the top one on my spiritual growth list that needs to be worked on. And I mean daily. My mouth can either be my best friend or my worst enemy. Sometimes it goes rogue, and I don't know how to stop it while other times it is full of wisdom and kindness, and I tell it, "Well, that was nice. Why can't you always be like that?" In reality it's just doing what my brain and heart tell it to. So in order to get it to say nice things, I need to get these truths to my brain and heart.

We know what we should say in certain situations, but it is getting this to happen more times than not that is the difficulty. If we want our words to be beneficial to others, then we need to fill our hearts with the very words we want to say. Getting them to stay in our hearts becomes the challenge. We do this by making it a daily habit of filling our minds with positive, helpful, and useful words. Out with the ugly words, in with the pleasant ones.

CHAPTER 2

Straight from the Heart

Before we even touch the subject of controlling our mouths, we need to address the area from the place they originate: the heart. Oh, the heart. So much feeling, so much love, so much joy, but also so much hurt, anger, hate, unforgiveness, regret, and pain. Our favorite thing to say as moms right now on social media is "My heart is full," letting everyone know that we are feeling content, loving towards our children or spouse at that moment in time or just plain happy.

Or how about, "That hurts my heart" or "My heart is aching"? As women we *love* to talk about the heart. Our society loves to ask us, "What does your heart tell you?" as an indicator of making decisions. Disney tells us, "A dream is a wish your heart makes." But God, as usual, says something in contrast to the world. Jeremiah 17:9 says, "The human heart is the most deceitful of all things and desperately wicked. Who really knows how bad it is?" (NLT)

Desperately wicked? Yikes. Who really knows how bad it is?? Ouch. Those are pretty harsh realities about a part of us that we deeply respect and listen to. If we always made decisions based on our feelings or "heart," we would have way more consequences than we already have. Our life's moments would change daily; sometimes hourly! We are full of emotions and feelings, sometimes really big feelings, and to let those rule our lives can quickly make things a mess.

But we can't always control our feelings. They rise up inside of us sometimes right on cue; other times unexpectedly. Our feelings are real, but that doesn't mean they are always right or good. The crucial aspect of our feelings is what we do with them. The most common way for those feelings to get out is through one of the smallest parts of our bodies: our mouths. This is the first place those feelings want to exit. It wouldn't hurt every once in a while to make those words wait at the doors of our mouths, so they can relax before we let them out; give them a once-over.

There are times when those feelings will produce good words of love and encouragement and pleasant things to hear, but there are those other times, for some of us more than we would like to admit, that those feelings produce hate, bitterness, jealousy, and selfishness. Our hearts are the first place those feelings are recognized. They are the place where they originate.

But we are the ones who get to choose what to do with them. Jesus said in Matthew 15:18, "But the things that come out of a person's mouth come from the heart…" See! I didn't make this up! Jesus, the Son of God, said it Himself: what comes out of our mouths comes from our hearts. So technically it's our hearts that are the culprits; the instigators of this whole word problem. And, Jesus is the boss, so you can't argue with Him.

We do though have the responsibility of what enters our hearts. Colossians 3:1 says, "Since, then, you have been raised with Christ, set your hearts on things above, where Christ is, seated at the right hand of God." We have the ability to "set our hearts" or focus them on what is right. Our hearts *are* where our words come from, but we have the self-control to decide what our hearts are focused on and what we let in them.

In Proverbs 4:23 it reads, "Above all else, guard your heart, for everything you do flows from it." God tells us to guard our hearts because He knows that it is the place where our words, actions, and thoughts flow from. We guard our hearts by being careful what we let in it which in turn fuels what comes out of our mouths. Or how about Proverbs 16:23 that says, "The hearts of the wise make their mouths prudent, and their lips promote instruction?" Right, there we see that learning wisdom will have our lips speaking instruction and good judgment. So what we are putting into our hearts is the key to what is going to come out of our mouths.

Here's another part of that responsibility. We get to decide what exits our hearts to the free world, our social media, our children and husband's ears, our coworkers, friends, extended family, the checker at the grocery store, that lady that's taking up the entire aisle with her cart (be gracious because I do that *a lot*. It's hard to pull my cart off to the side. I'm not perfect, people), the bank teller. You get it, right? I am going to assume that I am writing to people with brains and that you can finish this list and add to it whomever else is in your daily life that is going to hear your words.

Your words. Words that *you* are responsible for. Words that can change not only the person's day that you are talking to but your life as well. So when you hear the saying, "It came from the heart," that is more true than we know. Whether it is loving or mean, at that moment in time, those words came from the heart.

So let's recap a little bit before we go any further. First, we read in Jeremiah that our hearts cannot be trusted. They are deceitful and feel things that we don't tell them to because they have no brain and make mistakes. We then learned from Jesus himself that our hearts and minds are the breeding ground for feelings and are the source of our words.

So if we can't trust our hearts and they have the capability of deceiving us, then how can we always know that our words are going to come out the right way? Well, sometimes we can't know. Sometimes we truly think we are being helpful when we are not, hence, the deceptive part. But if we are careful and deliberate about what goes into our hearts, setting our hearts on the right things, we can better trust what is going to flow out of them. But that doesn't mean that we never say anything because we have a lot of important and lovely things to say to people. It just means that we need to be careful and think before we speak.

One of my favorite acronyms going around social media right now is this: Before you speak...*think!* T—is it true, H—is it helpful, I—is it inspiring, N—is it necessary, and K—is it kind. I just love this. It is so true. Our words have more power than any of us will ever know. So why not take some time to contemplate what we say, why we say it, to whom we say it, and how we can learn to sometimes just *not* say it.

I cannot even begin to count the times that I blurted out what I was thinking or feeling to then instantly wish I could hit rewind (for us souls who lived during the VHS days) or the back button and put those words right back where I had found them. There have been days when Groundhog Day seemed like a good movie to have come true in real life (also for those of us who were old enough to watch and enjoy a good movie in 1993). The thought of taking words back is a dream that all of us have. But we all know that it is literally impossible.

My goal in life is not to speak perfectly or always say the right words at the exact right time because, since I am a human in this flesh-suit, I am going to make mistakes and say things that are not always kind or helpful. But my goal *is* to lessen the hurtful words I do say and be very careful with what comes out of my mouth and whose hearts they land on. Because let me tell you something that you may not like: your words are going to land somewhere whether you like it or not. And, that my friends, is the gospel truth.

How about those times when we feel truth, love, encouragement, joy, excitement, laughter, singing, rising up in our hearts? And then the feeling of letting it out! Those are moments that we cherish and crave more of. There is nothing like saying something to someone at just the right time. There have been countless instances in my life where someone has said exactly what I needed to hear. Or the worship set at our church speaks right to me and my situation. I will be reading a book and instantly know that God has put it in my hand at that exact moment in time, for that exact season in my life.

Our words not only have power to harm, but they also have power to heal, encourage, lift up, care for, awaken, empower, remind, teach, fill up, create, and give life! I could go on and on. I love Proverbs 15:23 (NIV). It says, "A person finds joy in giving an apt reply—and how good is a timely word!" The New Living Translation says, "Everyone enjoys a fitting reply; it is wonderful to say the right thing at the right time!" Not only is the person hearing the words gaining something, but the speaker of those same words is too. It *is* wonderful to say the right thing at the right time just as much as it is amazing to hear the right words at the right time.

To be the one to encourage a new mom; tell your children you love them; compliment a friend or stranger on their outfit, hair, or make-up; thank your husband for his support and care for your family; tell a coworker how you admire their hard work; let your friend know how beautiful her voice is, brings us joy! When Jesus said it was more blessed to give than to receive, maybe He wasn't just talking about physical gifts but also the gift of words.

The same is to be said about receiving harsh words as much as it is to be the one to say them. Saying the wrong thing can lead to regret, hurt, remorse, bitterness, self-hate, and defeat. So while we may be directing our words towards someone else, they are affecting us just the same. Saying hateful, hurtful words is selfish but choosing to speak kind truths is selfless because it takes us out of the equation to lift up another person and to put the focus on them. The good feelings we feel in the process is just a bonus! It's like a reward for not only thinking of yourself.

Which, I guess if you focus on the reward, it takes out the whole goal of not doing it just for yourself... It's like the whole which-comes-first-the-chicken-or-the-egg thing. Let's not confuse ourselves too much or get into a theological conundrum. Say good things, and you will end up feeling good too. Say bad things, and you will end up feeling bad. There. Done.

CHAPTER 3

Interrupting

Who likes being interrupted when they talk? Anyone? Yeah, I didn't think so. No one likes it. It is the most frustrating thing to be right in the middle of a sentence or story and to have someone cut you off and totally disregard that you were talking first. For people who are quiet by nature, they let the other person take over even though they are irritated.

For people who like to talk (that would be me), we just keep talking until both stories are being spoken at the same time; each person getting louder to see who will be the winner! I am embarrassed to say that I have done this very thing many, many times. I have been on the winning and losing ends of those types of conversations. It makes me cringe just thinking about it. Do I still do it? Yes. I have not mastered this, but I am getting better and more aware.

Sadly, I wasn't really aware that I was doing this. But as I got older, I started noticing how much people were interrupting *me*! How rude! I would get so irritated and actually angry. I hated it so much that it seemed like everyone was doing it: close friends, family, strangers, my kids weren't letting me finish.

Then the cold, hard truth came: I started noticing it more in myself. I was the biggest culprit! Here I was so focused on how everyone else was interrupting me that I forgot to look at the only one I could control, and that was me. My husband's words, "You never let me finish" rang so loud in my head. I had been so quick to find this fault in others but didn't take the time to look to see if I was doing it.

I immediately started making it a point of waiting until the person that I was talking to was finished speaking. I actually did pretty well for a while. Then I started doing it again. And the first person to tell me was my husband. Crap! I thought I was doing alright at this. So, back to the drawing board. *Why* was I doing this? *Why* did I think it okay or at least out of habit; unknowingly start talking while someone else was? Those people had to feel the same way that I did. It was frustrating to say the least and downright rude. Plain and simple. I don't care what I had to offer to that conversation; it wasn't "my turn" as we would say in elementary school. I was "cutting in line" in front of someone else's thoughts and words.

Why do we interrupt? We obviously see their mouths moving and hear words coming out. We know how it feels. I know the easy answer is: we're human; we all make mistakes. I get that. But at some point, we need to do a little thing the Holy Spirit likes to call self-control. Don't argue with me. If you have a problem with it, argue with Jesus. It's in the Bible.

We can interrupt for a few reasons.

1. Excitement: we get super excited about what the topic is, and we absolutely cannot wait for the other person to finish.
2. Impatience: we think the other person is talking too slow or taking too long to get to the point, and we want to get out what we have to say.
3. Correcting: they aren't telling the story correctly or are giving the wrong information.
4. Irritation: we have heard that story a bajillion times, and if we hear it *one more* time…
5. Hurried: we have to go and don't have time to stay and listen, so we apologize and leave the conversation; hopefully explaining to them what we're doing as to not be rude.

6. Walking away: we see someone else or have other things on our minds that we literally walk away while that person is talking.
7. Questions: we need to ask a question to better understand what they're talking about.

I have done *every* single one. I have done these things to practically every person I know. And I have had them done to me. The excitement one: we get. When two women get together and are so excited and laughing, you almost don't care that the other one is interrupting. It's too exciting to not talk about! Our men *love* this about us. To be in a room with women who are talking and laughing over each other because of excitement just soothes their hearts. It's what they live for.

The questions one we get too. We want our listener to be engaged and to understand our story, so we're okay answering a few questions, so they can grasp what we're saying. These two are okay. They're understandable and don't sting. But the other five: not so fun. These hurt. And can make us mad, sad, and bad. (Who am I? Dr. Seuss?)

No matter what our intention is of interrupting someone else, they all stem from one thing: selfishness. We think that what we have to say is more important than waiting for the other person to finish talking. And more than likely are thinking of what to say *while* the other person is talking.

My words are so important that they need to be heard *right now*. My insight is better. My experience is beyond theirs. What could they possibly teach *me*? I am the expert on this topic. *Or* I know someone who is the expert which makes me know more than you. Isn't is just plain disgusting when we break it down bit by bit? We don't have to think that we are being selfish to be selfish. Even if we don't *mean* to be selfish, we still can be.

Interruption words most of the time are no less helpful and right and loving but just said at the wrong time. Everyone's words have value when they are right and loving and good. Most of us have amazing things to say about issues we know a lot about! But that doesn't give us the right to stop someone from saying their words just so we can say ours.

When your mouth starts opening, tell it "Wait your turn. Don't cut in line." King Solomon penned these words in Proverbs 29:20, "Do you see someone who speaks in haste? There is more hope for a fool than for him." Haste means to hurry or have an urgency of movement. When we interrupt, we are hurrying our words and have a sense of urgency to get our words out *before* listening.

I am still working on this one, you guys. Some days I'm killing it, but other days I can't keep my mouth shut at the right times. We're not going to be perfect at this, but we can get better. Now that I actually pay attention to this in me, I now pay attention to how others handle this and am always in awe of people who *do not* interrupt. I want to be like them when I grow up. Listening to someone is a gift. You are literally giving them something. You are extending a place for their voice to be heard whether it's joy, excitement and love or pain, hurt and worry.

Listening is a powerful character trait to have and exhibits maturity, discernment, and wisdom. Being a good listener is a trait that we look for in someone. It is an amazing thing to need a friend and know that they will listen. Even our children need someone to listen to them. Parenting and listening sometimes are hard to balance. As a parent, we know our kids need wisdom, instruction, and advice. But their opinions and ideas are just as important. We always say that we want our kids to talk to us. If that's the case, then we need let them do the talking and us do the listening sometimes. They're not going to want to talk to us if they know they won't be heard.

There's a great verse in James 1:19 that says, "My dear brothers, take note of this: Everyone should be quick to hear, slow to speak and slow to become angry." Do you see how the hearing part comes before the listening part? And how when we do speak we should be "slow to speak"?

James didn't write it in this order by accident. James and the people he was writing to were human too, not super-Christians. Their mouths were causing them and others trouble even back then. This kind of goes along with Proverbs 29:20 and not speaking in haste. If we are waiting to speak at the right time and listening, we won't be interrupting. Make a conscious effort to listen and wait your turn to talk. It will make such a difference in your communication with others *and* people will actually enjoy talking with you.

Make It Happen

1. *Prep yourself:* Before you go to work, to a lunch date with a friend, or even before you kids get up, tell yourself that you *will not* interrupt them and that you will listen. I know it doesn't seem like a massive action step but trust me. You would be surprised how preparing ahead of time, even with our words, will help you follow through. Set yourself up to *not* start talking while they are. Be prepared to possibly not get any words in edge-wise and to just be a listener. Coming from an obsessive talker—you will live through it. The world will keep spinning and everyone will come out of it alive. I promise.

2. *Sticky note:* Write down on a sticky note these words: *don't interrupt.* Put one on your bathroom mirror, on your computer or laptop for work, and on your steering wheel for those of you who are in your cars a lot for work.

3. *Truly listen:* If you are listening intently on what the other person is saying, you won't be planning ahead of what you're going to reply back as much. Soak in what they're saying. If you are doing this, your chances of interrupting are going to be a lot less.

4. *Apologize when you do interrupt:* Let's face it. You're going to do it again and again and again but hopefully fewer and fewer. You're not Mother Theresa. So when you do interrupt, stop right where you are and say you're sorry. Then let the other person finish.

CHAPTER 4

Gossip

I just hit a nerve. I know some of you are contemplating skipping over this chapter. Please don't. This isn't a call to perfection or accusations. I am not writing this as a self-righteous, shake-my-finger, soap-box moment. I am choosing this topic because of myself. "Hi, my name is Chessa, and I am a recovering gossiper." There, I said it. And every single one of you could say it too. Because we *all* have done it and will continue to mess up in this area. Don't try to deny it. Nothing gets past Jesus.

Most of us *love* to know what's going on. Our neighbors, friends, that one girl we went to high school with that's a lesbian now, that couple that is going through a divorce, that high school girl that got pregnant, the son or daughter that is addicted to drugs: you name the scandal, we want to hear about it.

We're like sharks smelling blood in the water the minute we hear of someone else's problems or—wait for it—someone else's success. Ouch. I've been there, too.

What is it that draws us to such curiosity that we can't keep our mouths or ears shut? Why do we feed off of other people's pain just to have something to talk about? The famous words, "Don't tell anyone, but…" make their way through a myriad of people who *promise* not to tell anyone but that one friend. Then the gossip-train takes off, and it becomes the game of telephone—the game we used to play when we were kids.

One person whispers something in another's ear then they whisper it to the next person and so on and so on. When it gets to the last person, they have to repeat out loud what was said, and it is *never* like the very first phrase that was whispered! Gossip is a lot if not exactly like the game of telephone. What is first told is never repeated exactly the same and just becomes a story that has been so changed and exaggerated; it isn't even close to the truth, *if* it was even truthful from the beginning.

One of my favorite verses on the mouth is Proverbs 10:19. The New Living Translation says it like this, "Too much talk leads to sin. Be sensible and keep your mouth shut." Woo-hoo! Those are *strong* words! Nothing like getting right to the point! I am pretty sure gossip would qualify as "too much talk," don't you think? Those conversations are rarely short.

How about this verse? Proverbs 11:13 says, "A gossip betrays a confidence, but a trustworthy person keeps a secret." When we confide in another person, we are telling them something that is so important to us. It is not something that we want the free world knowing otherwise it wouldn't be considered "confiding." We all know those women that talk about *everyone*. And, sadly enough, we sometimes get caught up in it.

What we really should be thinking is, "Do they talk about me like this?" The answer is yes, 99.9 percent of the time: yes, she talks about you like that especially if the person she is talking to you about is a good friend. And on the flip side, we know women that are vaults, steel traps, and will never repeat what we say to them. They know the importance of treasuring the information you have just shared with them and taking special care of it. We need to take a step back and be honest with ourselves. Which woman are we: the gossiper or the trustworthy person? Better yet, which one do we truly want to become?

Since Jesus told us that our words come from our hearts, let's dig into *why* we gossip, *why* we feel the need to listen to it, and dig into the roots of where our desire to do these things to others comes from.

Selfishness. Since every sin comes from selfish ambition as stated in James 3:16, we can easily start off with this reason. We are naturally selfish creatures. We are literally thinking about ourselves all day long. And this isn't always a bad thing. We need to feed ourselves, look presentable, exercise, eat healthy, drink water, get enough sleep, make money etc. There are a lot of things that have to do with ourselves that only we can do. We all get that. It's when we do things without thinking about the well-being of others and *only* ourselves that constitutes selfishness.

When we are listening to gossip or repeating gossip, we are not thinking about the person we are talking about. We are solely focusing on how much *we* want to hear the juicy news and how it makes *us* feel to be in "the know." Never, and I mean *never*, do we stop and think about how the person we are gossiping about would feel if they knew what we were saying. We distance ourselves from them and their problems. They just become that "girl" or that "guy" and not a flesh-and-blood person with real feelings. Since that person is not sitting directly in front of us, listening to our every word, we can distance ourselves from them and the situation; making easier to talk about them.

Jealousy. This word is just ugly. It causes us to think ugly thoughts, act ugly, and speak ugly words. Jealousy is so powerful that it can cause us to do things that we would never have done otherwise. We tend to gossip about those that we are jealous of. They have something we want whether a material item, career, baby, husband, new house, maybe good looks, great physique, or even just a likability that we wish we had.

The jealousy that starts in the heart sometimes makes it way out of the mouth as gossip. We put down the new thing they have as not as good as they say it is. We put down their ability to be a good mom with that new career or job they started. We find faults in their looks or character when they get chosen for that position we wanted or were honored for their hard work when we work hard too. We get jealous of our female peers when they start a new business because our dream is still stuck inside of us, and instead of being empowered and inspired, we find fault.

We gossip about them because we want what they have. But their success, their families, their dreams and visions, their bodies, their cars, houses, clothes, husbands, careers, whatever it is *does not belong to us*. It belongs to them.

We need to be happy for other women and celebrate them! I spent a lot of time in jealousy: wanting to look like other women; feeling threatened by some. It left me empty and miserable. Then I came across this verse one day: "A heart at peace gives life to the body, but envy rots the bone" (Proverbs 14:30). It can literally make you physically sick. I was tired of feeling like that! I was done with focusing on what others had instead of going for my own dreams and living out what God had called *me* to do, not what He called others to do.

So I made a decision that the second I started having any inkling of jealousy rising in my heart, I would shoot them a quick text *or* send them a note letting them know how amazing I thought they were and how excited I was for them. It took all of the focus off of me and put it on them. And guess what? It worked! Empowering and encouraging women to be their best not only fills them up but it fills us up, too!

Remember the phrase, "It is more blessed to give than to receive"? I know I have said it already, but I want it to be emblazoned in your hearts. *Give* encouraging words and jealousy will flee. Instead of gossiping about their supposed mistakes and faults or successes with others and wasting your words on hurt, use your words for encouragement, praise, and kindness! Your words may be exactly what they needed. And you will feel so much better for it. Jesus said you will be blessed.

Being nosy. Another word we use for a gossiper is nosy or a busybody because they are always in other people's business—wanting to know every new thing about everyone else. In the Bible we read, "We hear that some among you are idle and disruptive. They are not busy; they are busybodies" (2 Thessalonians 3:11). And again in 1 Timothy 5:13, "Besides, they get into the habit of being idle and going from house to house. And not only do they become idlers, but also busybodies who talk nonsense, saying things they ought not to." Notice the other word that is mentioned in these verses? Idle.

To be idle means to be lacking worth or basis or to not be occupied or employed. If you read chapter three of 2 Thessalonians, you will see how there were people who were idle or weren't working; taking other people's food and gossiping. They had nothing better to do because they were not employed, so their time and their words were lacking worth or basis. In fact, if you go to verse ten of that same chapter, Paul says, "The one who is unwilling to work shall not eat." Their unemployment and lack of hard work was causing them to be busybodies, nosy, and gossips. Working is a part of who we are. Without it, we are left to our own will. We become bored and need something to fill our time.

This is such a good word for us! If we are at work in our own lives, tending to our own children, our careers, our marriages, our friendships, serving others, staying in the Word, worshipping Jesus, and staying busy with what matters, we won't be idle—giving ourselves time to be concerned with other people's lives. Our words will not be lacking worth or basis if we are using them the way God intended.

Idleness is a breeding ground for gossip and worthless words. Reread 1 Timothy 5:13 again: "But also busybodies who talk nonsense, saying things they ought not to." Nonsense. Is that how we want our words to be known: as nonsense? Don't we all want our words to matter? God is showing us that if we sit around and do nothing, we may gravitate towards nosiness and talking about things that are none of our business.

We do not need to be inserting our opinions and "wisdom" into someone's story when it wasn't told to us to begin with. Unless you were asked to come alongside in a difficult season or even a monumental one, your words should be kept to yourself. Prayer should be the only words coming out of our mouths to the only One who can fix the situation, not gossip to someone who cannot.

And, if we feel the need to ask questions to anyone who might know anything just to fill our curiosity, then we need to get on our knees and ask God to close our mouths. Because here's another thing about gossip: we're not the only ones talking about that situation. So when our idleness and desire to know causes us to ask questions, *that* becomes gossip and gets repeated to the one with the problem in the first place! Just *asking* about the situation gives you the reputation of being nosy.

I think most of us know what it feels like to be on the receiving end of gossip. I was raised in a wonderful, Christian home. I truly can say that I have no complaints about my childhood except that I had to beg my mom and dad for $5, but when my brother, who was ten years younger and needed money in high school, my parents were literally throwing 20s at him. But it's neither here nor there…he was the baby. I get it now: they had more money with only one kid at home, blah, blah, blah. No hard feelings here.

So, back to my point. I really did love my childhood. I am the oldest of three children, and at the age of eleven, my parents bought a house that they would spend the next thirty years in. We went to church every Sunday. My mom was a stay-at-home mom, and my dad owned his own electrical business as a contractor. We lived in a great, small town in the central valley of California, and my dad was well respected in the building community.

I was a pretty average good girl that did some dumb things in high school. I drank a little on the weekends, didn't like to make my curfew very much, got okay grades, played sports, and got my first boyfriend when I was sixteen. I didn't do drugs, didn't steal, and had a fairly good reputation among my peers and teachers.

Then every high school parent's nightmare happened: I got pregnant. I had just turned seventeen when I found out during spring break of 1994. Looking back now, I can see how God timed mine and my sister's trip to Anaheim to visit my aunt and uncle perfectly. I found out when I was there keeping me and my boyfriend away from my devastated and hurt dad.

It took my father a week to finally accept the fact that I was going to be a mom, and when I got back from that trip in LA, he was ready and willing to support and help me through what would be an unexpected, to say the least, year. The help and support of mine and my boyfriend's family along with God's presence were hands down the biggest reasons that carried me through that.

And then the gossip began. What a perfect story for people to talk about. Nothing like a good little Christian girl getting pregnant in high school to spice up a girls' night or an after church, Sunday lunch. Rumors started flying that my neighbor was always seeing my boyfriend's truck at *all* hours in front of my house; staying the night. No wonder I got pregnant!

When in reality, my boyfriend wasn't even allowed to stay until midnight at my house, and we had to stay downstairs in full view of my parents and could *never* be alone. I am sure, all of the parents in town were questioning my mom and dad's parenting—making sure that everyone knew they would *never* let this happen to *their* kids!

Then there was the gossip at our school. And not just among the students mind you, but in the teacher's lounge. "Were we going to finish school and graduate?", "Was Chessa going to play sports anymore?" All of the questions and all of the rumors all about two young kids that most people didn't even know nor bothered to ask.

Our town was so small. I think it's fair to say that a fair amount of people had talked about me. I came back the beginning of my senior year and had my son on September 7, 1994. My boyfriend and I both graduated with our class; our son being nine months old at the time. We had proved all of the gossipers wrong. Fast forward to today. My son Michael is twenty-three, a father to my beautiful granddaughter, and my husband and I have been married for twenty years and had 3 more boys after we got married in 1997. These stories don't always end like this, but ours did and I am forever grateful.

Now let's rewind a few years back from today to 2011 and 2012. My husband and I went through some pretty bad stuff those two years. Our marriage was almost falling apart, and it was the scariest, most heartbreaking time of either of our lives. We lived in a different small town at the time; smaller than the one I grew up in.

We quickly became a gossiper's dream. Everyone began talking and even began asking our own children questions. Let's just say it was ugly all around, and the people that truly didn't care for us repeated whatever they had heard and it was hurtful. God restored and healed and saved our marriage. We are stronger than before and I thank God every day that he listened to our prayers and saved our family.

But part of the pain was the interference and nosiness of so many: adding to the damage. So not only do I know how it feels to gossip, but I know what it feels like to be the center of gossip: to have lies told about you and things to become so twisted. I know what it feels like to hear that someone is spreading rumors, hurt, and lies then have them smile straight to your face. Gossip causes nothing but pain and destruction.

Why are we always tearing each other down? We should be lifting each other up and encouraging one another. If we are so focused on someone else's failures and successes to the point that we "butt" into their stories uninvited then we aren't focusing on the right Person. When we are staring at Jesus, all of the competition, jealousy, nosiness, and insecurities fade away. They don't matter because He is the only thing that does. When we "set our hearts on things above, where Christ is seated at the right hand of God," as Paul tells us in Colossians chapter three, gossip will not come out of our mouths because our hearts will be filled with Christ. Our words will be love, compassion, empathy, kindness, gentleness, and humility.

After that incident, I vowed that I would not hurt anyone the way that I had been hurt. I told myself that it was none of my business what Susie and Sally were doing and I wouldn't care. I would remind myself of how gossip had affected me and that I wouldn't do that to someone else again. I would be a trustworthy woman who kept secret matters of my friend's hearts to myself. If someone said, "Please don't say anything," I would honor it. I didn't want to be known as a gossiper. Because no matter what we hear, true or not, it's not our story to tell. Plain and simple.

Make It Happen

1. *Pray*: Specifically, ask God to help you keep your mouth *shut* to empathize with others in their pain, to not want to listen to gossip, and to look at the person being talked about the way God does. It is not his will for you to gossip, so when you pray, have faith that He will come through on this.

2. *Walk away*: If you do not feel strong enough to *not* gossip, politely excuse yourself from the conversation. Do this however you can, not lying about where you are going of course, but physically exit the conversation.

3. *Change the subject*: When you feel the conversation going to gossip-mode, try and change the subject. "Oh my gosh! Kelly! I totally forgot to ask you about your dinner the other night!" or "You guys, I don't want to change the subject (even though that's exactly what you're going for here) *but* I need your advice on potty training." (insert your issue here. We all have them.)

4. *Remind yourself that you are not getting the whole story*: Since you are not hearing it "from the horse's mouth," chances are you are getting the story ten people deep and probably not even close to the truth.

5. *Put yourself in the person's shoes*: How would you feel if you had to deal with that situation? Would you repeat what you are saying to that person's face if they were standing in front of you? How would you feel if they were talking about you like this?

6. *Be bold*: This step might not be for everyone, but if you're bold enough simply say, "I don't want to talk about ———, you guys. It's really none of our business." If you are brave enough to take this step, which I highly recommend, the chances of someone telling you some good gossip is going to go down drastically. It's hard to gossip to someone when they don't want to listen; it takes the fun out of it for them.

CHAPTER 5

Wisdom

We can usually tell if a person has wisdom or not. How can we tell? By their words. Talking with people can tell us a lot about them even if they are not talking about themselves. Yes, their actions can show wisdom too, but the words they are speaking can be so revealing. Being wise is something that I think most of us strive for.

Once we get past high school and into the "real world", so to speak, we start realizing that knowing things becomes extremely important. Wisdom becomes obvious to have when choosing a partner to spend your life with or friends to hang out with. When we start families and raise kids we desperately seek wisdom from anywhere and anyone that will help! Starting that new job or career calls for learning and gaining knowledge and experience which turns into wisdom.

Everywhere we turn, we are always making decisions that can directly affect, not only the outcome of our day, but the outcome of our lives. Life can be tough and lacking wisdom can only add to the difficulties. But to gain wisdom and discernment literally gives life and peace to ourselves and those around us.

How do we get wisdom? Where do we start? James tells us in chapter one verse five, "If any of you lacks wisdom, you should ask God, who gives generously to all without finding fault, and it will be given to you." God gives us wisdom. And all we have to do is ask and believe that He can give it to us. That's it. And He gives it to us generously. He wants us to have wisdom and discernment. He doesn't want us to just wing it for the rest of our lives. He doesn't want us to not know how to handle difficult situations.

As parents, we want our children to grow in their understanding, to keep learning from their mistakes, and make good decisions in every area of their lives. God looks at us the same! He loves to see us learn from our failings, gain wisdom, and make better choices. In Proverbs 23:23, we are instructed to "get the truth and never sell it; also get wisdom, discipline, and good judgment. The father of godly children has cause for joy. What a pleasure to have children who are wise." When we walk in wisdom and good judgment, it makes our Father happy just like when our children do when they make good choices and listen to our guidance and understanding. Wisdom is a blessing to receive and to give away.

The older I get, the more I realize how much I don't know. I am sure you either feel the same way or have heard this saying before. It is so true. When I was in high school, I thought I knew everything and, of course, way more than my parents. In my twenties, I *really* knew more than my parents and the world. I was young and hip and had all of the answers.

We had our first home, a couple of kids, we weren't doing too bad for being a young family. My 30s started out with some doubts of if I knew what I thought I knew. I had four kids by then and my first was starting middle school. I still knew more than my mom and dad at this point in time and was pretty confident that our child-rearing was going fantastic. We had gotten three through potty training; number four took a little longer than I had hoped, but we can't have it all. I was going to know *everything* my boys did because "I had already done it", and nothing was going to get past me like it had my mom when I was rebellious. Of course it wouldn't: I knew more than all of them. Obviously.

Then my older son hit high school. Fun times. Actually, it was pretty fun most of the time. Teenagers can be very enjoyable truth be told. They also can be real jerks and do some really dumb stuff. He soon taught me that I didn't really know everything and that I had a lot to learn. I started doing what I think most parents with teenagers do at least once in their lives: I called my parents and apologized to them. I told them I was sorry for everything horrible I had done to them. Every lie, every missed curfew, every haughty and snotty reply, the drinking—everything.

I humbly realized that I had been a jerk myself. Chessa, the know-it-all, didn't know as much as she thought she did. The biggest lesson I learned in my mid 30s was that I *did not* know everything. And I had three more boys to go! I started wanting, no, *craving* wisdom. I wanted it and I wanted it bad. Parenting is hard, and I wanted to do it as best as I could. My prayers quickly and strategically became focused on wisdom, wisdom, wisdom. I wanted as much as I could get. I even began calling my mom and mother-in-law for help and advice. And guess what? That verse in James came true.

When I would ask for wisdom, God would give it to me. Sometimes it would come in the form of a book I was reading, sometimes a song, or other times a friend's advice. There were also times when he gave it to me through my husband. There were moments when God would just tell me exactly what I needed to do and say. I didn't always like what I heard and sometimes had to be told multiple times before I actually acted on it. I either just wanted to make sure it was from God before I did it or silently hoped for another answer. Because wisdom is not always easy to carry out, but it always works. God always wants us to walk in wisdom, to make hard decisions with it, and most importantly to *speak* it.

As we have been learning, whatever our hearts are filled with is what will come out in our words. So if our hearts are filled with wisdom then our words will be filled with wisdom too. Wisdom and discernment are not only helpful to our own situations but also to those who come to us for advice, instruction, and encouragement.

Speaking wisdom to someone or over their situation is one of the ways that we speak life. When we have insight into a problem, we can give life to a person that may be experiencing a similar one. Being an older mom, I have had younger moms or women with children younger than me ask me my opinion or knowledge in a certain area.

I would not be able to impart any wisdom if I did not already have it in my heart.

Staying in God's Word and spending time with Him is the number one way we gain wisdom. Proverbs 4:5 says, "Get wisdom, get understanding; do not forget my words or turn away from them." In chapter five verse one, we read, "My son, pay attention to my wisdom, turn your ear to my words of insight." By reading the words of wisdom given to us by God, we get wisdom and understanding. By them we gain the knowledge and discernment we need to navigate through life. The older I get, the more I listen and appreciate the wisdom from those who have lived longer than me or who have experience in an area that I do not.

We have all tried to "figure things out on our own" and sometimes that is okay. Certain things can only be learned by trial and error, but there is a lot of heartache that could be avoided by listening to wisdom. I cannot even count the number of times that if I had just asked for wisdom, I would have suffered a lot less; sometimes, not at all. Since none of us are perfect, we almost always gain wisdom from our life experiences. What we do with our mistakes and/or hurts is what can create wisdom in us.

To learn from our failures is the first step towards our knowledge in wisdom. If we cannot or, for some of us, will not learn from our downfalls, we will more than likely repeat them. Gaining the discernment from our experiences is what fills our hearts. That wisdom is what we can pour out to those who need it. If no lesson is learned, that defeat, that pain can't be used to benefit someone else or ourselves. The worth of sound judgment coming from our past hurts goes far beyond us. It can be used for great things.

The words we use to tell our stories and what we learned from them have such an unbelievable impact! Our past becomes the answer to someone's present; our wisdom becomes their liberation; our being raw and real, no matter how painful to retell the story, becomes a part of their story. What we have gleaned, we need to freely give.

For some of us this can be hard. To tell another of your past mistakes means being vulnerable and showing your weaknesses. It means opening your heart up to possible judgment and rejection. Fear can start to rise up extinguishing the desire of wanting to warn or encourage the person in front of you. Some of the wisdom we've gained was in ways we wish we hadn't. We may have been betrayed by someone close to us or have been the one that did the betraying and hurting.

So to offer our advice may mean showing faults we would rather keep hidden inside. And there does need to be wisdom in what we reveal and to whom we reveal it. If we prayerfully consider whether or not we should share our story, God will show us the right time to come alongside that specific person or maybe group of people.

If we choose to let our story out, we choose light over darkness. We break down walls of insecurity, self-doubt, and condemnation. We expose the lies that tell others they will never get free of their failures or shame or that there are no answers. People need to hear from others and how they came out of the other side alive and healthy. Speaking wisdom can and will send the enemy running. He hates wisdom. Wisdom to the devil is like kryptonite. When we are listening to what draws us to a life of understanding and peace, his grip on our situation gets weaker and weaker.

Knowing what God says in His Word and saying it out loud shows Satan how much power he can and cannot wield. Our words are not only powerful to those we are offering wisdom to but are also mighty against any scheme our enemy will try and bring against us. And, then like Joseph, we can say to the devil and to our past mistakes, "You intended to harm me, but God intended it for good to accomplish what is now being done, the saving of many lives" (Genesis 50:20, NIV). Those many lives are those you have spoken to and will speak your words of wisdom to.

What happens when we do not choose to learn wisdom, knowledge, and understanding? I mean, we have a choice to walk away from wisdom. It isn't something that just implants itself in our hearts. We have to want it, search for it, and when we find it, settle it deep within our souls. We need to let it take root, grow, and become a natural way that we act and speak.

In Proverbs 21:16 we read, "The wise in heart are called discerning, and gracious words promote instruction," and again in verse 23, "The hearts of the wise make their mouths prudent, and their lips promote instruction." But in Proverbs chapter fifteen in verse seven, we see the opposite of what wisdom produces. It says, "The lips of the wise spread knowledge, but the hearts of fools are not upright." A few verses down in fourteen we read, "The discerning heart seeks knowledge, but the mouth of a fool feeds on folly."

We can see a pattern of hearts that are set on knowledge and prudence produce wise words and that foolish hearts, or hearts that want nothing to do with wisdom, are not upright or godly. In fact, we are not only told to not be foolish and to seek knowledge and discernment, but we are instructed to stay away from fools. "Stay away from a fool, for you will not find knowledge on their lips. The wisdom of the prudent is to give thought to their ways, but the folly of fools is deception." Wise people pay attention to what they are doing and saying, but a fool's ways are deceptive. Senseless people are not conscientious to their actions and are not mindful of what their words will affect.

Wisdom makes choices that have life-giving consequences. It can be the hardest thing to hear or the hardest thing to speak. It speaks God's truth into difficult situations and gives answers that are sometimes hard to handle. There are times when wisdom doesn't tell what we want to hear; when the answer goes against our flesh. Even though the words we may be hearing are what is best, that doesn't mean that they will pleasant to accept.

That also goes for when we are the ones speaking understanding to someone else. Just because God has given us the right thing to say in no way means the person we are communicating it to will listen. Words of wisdom have to be accepted into someone's heart for it to actually take effect. We can have just the right words at the just the right time.

Our experience could be far greater making our words helpful to that person, but if they do not listen and act on that wisdom, it won't matter. If it's not what they were hoping to hear, they are forfeiting wise advice that could be theirs. We do not have control over how our friend, son, daughter, spouse, sibling, whoever it is you are trying to impart wise council to, responds to our words.

Our job is to speak truth and understanding when we feel God is leading us to. If we ask Him, He will not only give us the words to say but also when to say it. The timing of our words is actually sometimes more important than the words themselves. If it's not said at the right time, their hearts might not be ready to receive it like they would at a different moment.

Another reason: as we see in scripture that people are not ready to listen is because their hearts are still foolish. They won't accept discernment or do not want it because actually applying the knowledge given to them will mean giving up whatever it is that is stunting their growth. One of the most frustrating things I can think of is when someone will not listen to advice. It is nerve-racking and so hard! You know what the end game is for them on the other side of that horrible decision, but they will not listen. It's during those times that you hope they will learn from their mistake that has not yet happened.

But we still love and guide and wait for the right moment when our words will can be used for good. And good ole King Solomon had something to say about that too. "Listen to the words of the wise; apply your heart to instruction. For it is good to keep these sayings in your heart and always ready on your lips" Proverbs 22:17–18. Listen, apply, and be ready.

Why should we want wisdom? What benefits are there from having it, learning it, and speaking it to others? Well, for obvious reasons everyone wants wisdom. Wise people seem smart, and we want to be smart. We do not want anyone thinking we are dumb or that we don't have it together. But overall wisdom is something that we all know is beneficial to how we live our lives.

We all should be growing in maturity and wisdom even if that growth is painful. Those life experiences grow our discerning muscles to help us in future situations. Listening and learning from those who have been in our shoes and actually applying the strength they are gifting us. Because that is what wisdom is a gift.

There is a wonderful and revealing description of wisdom in Proverbs 3:13–18 (NIRV). It reads:

> Blessed is he who finds wisdom.
> Blessed is the one who gains understanding.
> Wisdom pays better than silver does.

She is worth more than rubies.
Nothing you want can compare with her.
Long life is in her right hand. In her left
hand are riches and honor.
Her ways are pleasant ways. All her paths
lead to peace.
She is a tree of life to those who hold her close.
Those who hold on to her will be blessed.

First of all, can we just appreciate the fact that wisdom in the book of Proverbs is likened to a "woman" or in some versions a "lady"? When I read these verses, I imagine a woman with a graceful demeanor, classy but not stuffy, not anxious or worried about life, fun, easy to approach, kind, gentle, and happy. I admire this woman and want to be like her. Don't you want this to be said of you? To embrace wisdom and have it so deep in your heart that it radiates off of you?

I love this set of verses because they tell us the worth of wisdom. They tell us what we can have when we find it. When we find wisdom and discernment, we are blessed. The worth of having insight is worth more than rubies! The return we receive for gaining wisdom is superior to money, silver, jewels, and nothing that we will ever want can be matched.

To be wise means to walk on a satisfying, right, and peaceful path. As a general rule, if we choose wisdom, we can have a long life and riches and honor. People will respect and trust your words because you have been proven to speak truth. And verse eighteen says that if we hold her (wisdom) close, it will be like a tree of life. When we are making decisions based on God's Word, choices that benefit us, that are not damaging, our chances of living a prolonged life are much higher.

Why would it say that wisdom is better than wealth then the following verse says that she can give us riches? Because we can obtain riches and wealth by being wise in the way we work for and manage our money. There are many biblical principles that instruct us on how to administer our finances. But even though we may have silver, gold, money, or jewels, wisdom is still by far superior. And to know that every single one of us has access to this understanding and that God yearns for us to have it, to live our lives in pursuit of what is right and what will keep us on the path closest to Him, is amazing.

Just about every situation we will conduct ourselves in will need our words whether written, texted, or spoken, so it would be always in our good interests and the interests of others to use our words wisely. When we speak, our words flow out to every area of our lives. Whether wise or foolish, our speech is literally saturating the atmosphere around us and into the minds and hearts of our listeners. Our words have impact and influence.

In today's culture, we have a myriad of ways and opportunities to get our words out into the world. We live in a society that feels the need to constantly speak their minds and vomit those feelings onto posts and live chats, emails, and blogs. And, don't get me wrong, I love these avenues! Some of the best advice and wisdom I have received was on a podcast or Instagram. But how we use them is the question.

This has become one of the best representations of our culture and sometimes the worst. This is the very reason why in a world where anyone and everyone has a voice, be the voice of truth, humility and grace because at the heart of all of those is wisdom.

Be the wise voice in a sea of foolishness—standing out against voices that lead people away from truth. Let your words lead them closer to what is right and good, peaceful, and loving. Use them to draw people to a life that is built on learning from experience and listening to those who have been there. Teach the ones who are entering the very situation you just left if they will let you. Our words teach, and you are the only one who gets to decide what yours prepare and train your listeners for.

The road to wisdom is never easy. Sure, there are mile markers of learning from another person's mistakes, close calls, and even lessons in easy moments. But most of them are marked with pain, heartache, shame, and defeat. The final defeat is when we do not do anything with them: when we shove the pain down and let the enemy win.

If you let Him, God will use the rough places and turn them into healing, joy, redemption, and victory. That's when it becomes better than rubies, gold, silver, and wealth. Wisdom is almost always earned the hard way. Most of mine was acquired in ways I wish it hadn't been. That hard road matures our hearts and eventually highlights the best decisions and paths to take. It reminds us of the past and emboldens us to make our future look different than where we have been.

Although we would rather forget our mistakes and pray that our onlookers would get amnesia during our worst moments, it is the memory of the past wounds that keep us in line. A wise person doesn't forget no matter the pain. They use it for theirs and other people's good. They do not shame themselves. They accept grace and forgiveness. They do better than they did before and guard themselves. They speak it to whoever will listen. That's what wisdom is for us: mistakes, learning, forgiveness, changing, and teaching.

Babies are not born with wisdom and insight. They cannot speak knowledge nor can their sweet little brains understand anything but food, physical touch, and warmth. It is "living" that shows us what to do and what not to do. It is all of our hours, days, weeks, months, and years that feed wisdom. It is a process: a course in growth and progression. We are all in school—learning—and if we apply what we have picked up along the way, we all can become teachers.

We all have something to offer. Don't let your history be wasted. Use it for God's Kingdom, where grace is the native language. We are all broken. It's the ones who were put back together that need to lead. We just have to give our mistakes to God, be in His Word, and allow His wisdom to saturate our hearts and minds.

I am sure you have noticed that most of the verses I have shown you are from the book of Proverbs. It is a book full of great wisdom which still holds true for us today and can be used in any situation. The author of the majority of Proverbs was written by King Solomon, King David's son. 1 Kings 3 tells us the story of how Solomon became so wise and where he gained the wisdom to pen the book of Proverbs and Ecclesiastes.

If we start in verse five of chapter three, we see that God actually came to Solomon and spoke to him. It says, "At Gibeon the Lord appeared to Solomon during the night in a dream, and God said, 'Ask for whatever you want me to give to you.'" God had given Solomon the choice to have whatever he wanted. Anything. Can you imagine? The Creator of everything asking his creation what it wants.

Solomon replies and in verses 7–9 says, "Now, Lord my God, you have made your servant king in place of my father David. But I am only a little child and do not know how to carry out my duties… Your servant is here among the people you have chosen, a great people, too numerous to count or number. So give your servant a discerning heart to govern your people and to distinguish between right and wrong. For who is able to govern this great people of yours?"

Solomon could have asked for anything, and he chose to ask for discernment. He understood that he could not live his life and be the king the people of Israel needed without God and His guidance. Solomon had set his heart on God and believed that God's ways were better than his own.

> The Lord was pleased that Solomon had asked for this. So God said to him, 'Since you have asked for this and not for long life or wealth for yourself, not have asked for the death of your enemies but discernment in administering justice, I will do what you have asked. I will give you a wise and discerning heart, so that there will never have been anyone like you, nor will there ever be.' (1 Kings 3:10–12)

If you keep reading, God even gave him the things that Solomon didn't ask for! He gave him wealth and honor and no other king would be equal to him in his lifetime.

Solomon's answered request for wisdom is still living today: in God's Word. *We* have access to this wisdom given to Solomon by our God. And, more importantly, we have access to the same God that Solomon spoke to that night. The same God that gave him this wisdom is the very same God that James told us to ask for our wisdom from.

We may never be a renowned queen of a nation of people or have all the wealth in the world, but we can live out our days on this earth with wisdom—making great choices for ourselves and our families. Those words of insight and right judgment are words that we can speak today. They are for us and our families. They are for our friends and neighbors. We can share and put voice to these verses anywhere and everywhere. Our words can be full of wisdom if we choose them to be.

Make It Happen

1. *Read the Bible*: Do not let God's Word intimidate you. God's desire is for you to read and understand His Word. Just ask Him, and He will help you to enjoy, grasp, and even crave His book. Why would He ever ask us to do something that was not attainable without His help? This is where He wants you to be; where He always meets us. It is power, life, and His very words for *everyone*, not just the theological graduates and pastors on Sunday mornings. If you are not familiar with the Bible, it's okay! Start in the book of Proverbs or the book of Mark. Read a few verses or a full chapter. But just start! Once you fill your heart with God's wisdom, it will start to manifest in your words.

2. *Learn from your mistakes*: This very cliché statement couldn't be more true. Take an honest look at your life habits. If you keep making the same mistakes and don't seem to be learning, you probably do not have wisdom in that area. Write down the things that you can't seem to get right—no matter how big or small. Try a different option than what you have been doing. Gain wisdom by not repeating the same steps that lead you down the path of pain and regret. Get help if you need it and learn wisdom from someone who has been there.

3. *Teach others*: Teaching comes in so many forms. You don't have to be standing in front of a group of students or adults to be a teacher. Ask God who needs your wisdom, so you can use your past to help build someone's future.

CHAPTER 6

Self-Talk

What are you saying to yourself? Are they reminders of past mistakes, shame, or hate? Is it encouragement, hope, and praise? How about comparison or doubt? Are you unintentionally spreading fear into your heart and mind? Whether we pay attention to it or not, we are talking to ourselves all day long.

Our beliefs, who we hang out with, where we work, what we listen to, and what we read, all affect what we tell ourselves. And what we tell ourselves turns into where we are going; who we become. Self-talk can be one of the most influential or destructive voices we listen to. Since we are the only ones listening, we are free to say what we want; never thinking about the consequences. Did you know that there were consequences to what you tell yourself? We normally think they only come when we act or speak to others, but our words and thoughts to only us can have life altering effects.

Ever hear the saying, "You are what you believe"? Or "You are what you say you are"? These hold more truth than we realize. Our thoughts become who we are. Those thoughts come from our upbringings, experiences, feelings, people we choose to be around, music we listen to, and what we read. Everything we decide to input into our minds and hearts is what we become.

Did you notice that I used the words "choose" and "decide"? That's because *you* have the power to say what goes in and what comes out. *You* determine the people you are around and the information that you soak up. *You* get to pick what you believe which turns into what you speak over your life. *You* have the amazing responsibility to determine your self-talk.

Most of us would never say to our closest friends and family what we would say to ourselves. We more than likely wouldn't say those things to complete strangers. Yes, there are truths and suggestions that sometimes come out of our mouths that 100 percent line up with what we are telling ourselves, but there are more things that we say to only us that would never let hit our listener's ears.

We are so happy to encourage our friend to go after that job they want or to take a risk on an exciting venture or relationship. We see them thinking and talking about their dreams, and we try to inspire them to keep going. We compliment them on a job well done or even as simple as a cute outfit or new hairstyle. We boost their self-esteem; helping them to believe they can do anything they set their minds to!

Then we wake up every morning, see our dreams out in the distance, tell ourselves it's too late, there's no way it will happen, and that it is unrealistic. Staring at our reflections in the mirror and our clothes in the closet, we remind ourselves that we are not like the thirty fitness women we follow on Instagram. As mothers, we compare our parenting skills and involvement in our children's activities and schools with everyone else—even though their families and careers look much different than ours. We beat ourselves up over our mistakes and let fear control our decisions.

Do any of these look familiar?

- I can't forgive myself
- What if I fail?
- I am not worthy.
- I am afraid.
- I am ugly.
- No one likes me.
- I am stupid.
- I have already tried and failed too many times.

- I am not educated.
- I am too loud.
- She's a better mother than me.
- I am too quiet.
- I am not capable.
- I will never be free of this
- I am not strong enough.
- I am fat
- I can't do it
- It's too hard

"I can't," "I'm not," "I won't," "I'll never," "them," "they," "what if." These words plant seeds that grow down deep and become negative—inhibiting us to be all that God has created us for. Would you say any of these things to your best friend or child? I know there are some who would, but I believe that the majority of mankind would not.

If you answered no, then why would you speak these things to yourself? What makes someone else more deserving than you? What we speak is what we act out. It is what we accept. These statements start to mold us and our decisions every day. And, if we do not stop saying them, we will never reach for our finest life: the only life that we are given.

Do not let the "what ifs" take root in your dreams and the "I cant's" keep you tethered down. We settle because we think we're not ready or capable. We see other people accomplishing what we want but believe the myth that those achievements are for more worthy and educated people. Your words will dictate your life. They will cripple you if you let them. They will make you a prisoner of what you don't want and a settler in the land of unfinished desires.

But what if you spoke on purpose? What if you decided to choose your words carefully and intentionally? You have the capability to pick out what you are going to say to yourself, you know. You are just as important as your friend that needs encouragement to finish school, eat right, lose weight, run that marathon, stay strong during the adoption process, work hard on their failing marriage, and feel beautiful, wanted, and important. Reassuring words are not just for others; they are for you too. Support doesn't just come from outside voices; they need to come from you, to you, and for you! See? It *is* okay to talk to yourself!

From my earliest childhood memories, I had anxiety. My parents and I did not know what it was at the time, and so we just chalked it up as me being a "hypochondriac": someone who was afraid of everything. I remember being terrified and thinking my heart was going to beat out of my chest. I always thought something was wrong with me. I would feel a terror rise up in me, and instantly, my heart would race. I was certain that I would have a heart attack.

My dad would have to come pick me up from sleepovers because in an instant panic would fill my body and I would need to go home immediately. It followed me into high school, and I would have panic attacks for no reason. My early twenties proved no different. I would have an anxiety attack literally every morning on my twenty-minute drive to work and every evening on my twenty-minute drive home. Every single day.

No one but my mom knew. I was too embarrassed to tell my husband. He was so strong emotionally and never seemed to have any fear. I did not want him or anyone else thinking I was weak. My anxiety got so bad that I started not being able to leave my house. I would cancel playdates with friends if it meant I had to drive out of town, and I always had to have my mom or sister with me in the car when I took long drives or even to the next town ten minutes away

I don't think I ever went to one of my children's or my own doctor's appointments by myself for years. It was pure torture. It got to the point that I didn't even know what I was afraid of anymore. The attacks themselves became the center of my fears.

One night, while I was at church with my boys, I felt a panic attack coming. I looked back at my mom, who was sitting behind me, and told her I had to leave right then. She knew what I had meant and understood why. When I got home, my husband who had stayed home because he was sick was lying down on the couch. As I walked through the door, he looked at me and said, "Oh no, are you sick now too?"

I shook my head, sat down on the couch next to him, and immediately started crying. I couldn't do it anymore. I needed to tell him.

I was twenty-six, and we had been together since we were sixteen. I started to explain my anxiety disorder and all of the fear that I had been living with since I was a little girl. I revealed how debilitating it was and how I had actually fought through panic attacks while in the car with him, and he had never known I was having one.

Writing this makes me want to cry. I was so broken. Panic disorder is one of the most excruciating emotional things a person can go through. Looking back at all of the years, I had believed that it would never go away and that I was destined to suffer in that way until I died; breaks my heart.

My husband didn't react the way I had thought he was going to. He did not think I was weak. He actually didn't know what to say because he didn't understand. He just stared at me with a sad expression and said he was so sorry. There truly was nothing he could do; nothing anyone could do. After I told him, I went into the bathroom, ran myself a hot bath, and cried for about an hour. I couldn't live like this anymore. I felt trapped and confined to a life that had no hope or room to be who I wanted to be or go where I wanted to go.

Panic and anxiety were in control, and they told me how far I could move and who I was going to become. I would like to tell you that after that hot bath, I started my upward climb out of my misery, but I didn't. After a scare at the gym one morning with my heart beating irregularly, I sent myself into a full-blown panic attack, and an employee had to call 911.

When the ambulance arrived, I had calmed down and my heart had gone back to beating normal. But when they started taking my blood pressure and heart rate, I got extremely nervous and had another attack.

The EMT looked up at me with a strange look and said, "Are you okay? How is your breathing?" I answered back that I was fine but was nervous because I did not like anything remotely associated with the medical field especially if it had to do with me.

"Why?" I had asked him.

The EMT explained that my heart rate had gone from 70 beats per minute to 150 beats per minute in literally seconds. Great. Now they wanted to take me to the hospital. After a meeting with the ER doctor and then a cardiologist, I was given a wonderful diagnosis of SVT, super ventricular tachycardia. That's a really fancy name for a fast heart rate. The upper chamber of my heart that was supposed to be pacing my heart rate was not doing its job.

Perfect. Now my anxiety issues had a name. Guess what set in? You guessed correctly: panic. I ended up having more attacks the month that followed than I had been having before the gym incident.

I told myself that there was something wrong with me. My mind flooded with the terror of not being able to control my anxiety at all. No amount of deep breathing or preparation was going to help. I had a condition and now a cardiologist at the age of twenty-six. My husband had even ended up calling 911 twice in one month because I was sure my heart was going to explode and I was going to die right there.

I truly thought I was never going to see my boys or husband because I wouldn't be there. And, if I am going to be honest, I thought that being dead would have been easier because then I wouldn't have to feel panic again. I would be in Heaven with Jesus. This is how bad it had gotten.

Then one day, I had enough. I started to get mad. What had happened to me? Who was I? I couldn't function normally, and my thoughts were filled with fear and worry. My anxiety had hit an all-time high. I was never going to be able to leave my house again without a full-blown attack. This was ridiculous! I wanted to drive to the next town and meet a friend for lunch or take my boys to the park or shopping (actually, no, I did not want to take them shopping. That was a horrible thing to do with my boys at the time), or go get my hair done without the fear of hyperventilating. I wanted my life back, but I didn't know how to do it.

I had prayed and begged more times than I can count that God would take this away from me. I knew He didn't want me to suffer in this way, so why was it not leaving? I wanted to be the strong, confident woman that I had been portraying to everyone. I was tired of feeling helpless and scared. I was too young to be stuck, not only in my house, but in every aspect of my life. I could not move forward if I was being held down by anxiety.

Then one day when I was deep in prayer, asking God, yet again, for a miracle—for Him to make this weight leave me for good—I felt Him gently speak to me. I wish it would have been an audible voice, but maybe He knew it would have sent me into a panic attack, and that was the very thing I was trying to avoid.

God almost always speaks to me with a gentle nudge in my thoughts. I heard him explain to me that He would help me but I needed to start helping myself. He wanted me to take control of my thoughts. He wanted me to look at the attacks for exactly what they were: attacks from the enemy. He wanted me to go to His word and get my answers there. So that is what I did.

After God revealed His answer to me, I started exactly where the power was at—the Bible. I looked up verses on fear and anxiety and literally wrote them down and memorized them. I memorized 2 Timothy 1:7 (NKJV), "For God has not given us a spirit of fear, but of power and of love and of a sound mind."

I wrote Philippians 4:6–7 on a 3x5 notecard and took it with me wherever I went. This became my anchor verse during that season. "Do not be anxious about anything, but in every situation, by prayer and petition, with thanksgiving, present your requests to God. And the peace of God, which transcends all understanding, will guard your hearts and your minds in Christ Jesus."

This was my answer. This was the truth that I needed to tell myself. My self-talk had been fear, panic, hopelessness, and lies. I had believed a lie, and because I had believed it, I started speaking it to myself. I became what I was saying. I was a panic-ridden, fearful, and desperate woman who could see no way out. I had told myself that I would be in this state forever and that it was just who I was: a part of me. There was no cure.

Looking back, I love how God didn't just take my anxiety away the moment I asked him. At the time, that is what I wanted so badly from Him, but He knew what I needed and the journey that I had to go through to strengthen my faith. He wanted me to fight and overcome with His word and my belief in Him. So the hard work began.

I wrote down what I would tell myself when I woke up in the middle of the night with a panic attack. I prepared to fight because that is what I was doing: fighting for my freedom. On a piece of paper, I wrote down truths. I would speak them out loud even if they didn't feel right. I told myself that I was going to be fine, that there was nothing wrong with me and I was not going to die, that the attack would end, and that God was with me.

How many attacks had I gone through the past twenty years, and I was still alive? What I began telling myself was what I started to believe and is who I became. I fought against lies with truth. I had to retrain my mind and kill the self-defeating talk that had taken over. My anxiety attacks didn't end that day or even that month, but they became less and less until eventually I wasn't having them at all.

My words and the Word of God Himself had power over my situation. I was choosing my words on purpose and deliberately. They took shape in my mind until there was no more room for panic. I am grateful to say that I have been anxiety disorder free for seven years now. It was not easy, but I grew spiritually, and God taught me the authority of His Word and the great influence my own words had.

Are you in a battle that you feel you will never win? Are you settling for a version of your life when you aspire for more? I am going to almost guarantee it is because of your self-talk. You have a dialogue tailored for certain situations. Your mind is on auto and defaults to discouraging and mediocre thoughts. You will never move on from this position because you're not telling yourself anything different!

That is exactly what I had done. I was settling for anxiety because I truly believed I would have to suffer through it for the rest of my existence. I only started overcoming my fears when I started speaking truth against them. I was determined that I would not live a life of panic and fear. I was tired of coming to an agreement with the enemy. I was agreeing with the devils plan for my life, not my Father's. My arrangement with the liar had come to an end. He would have no say over whether or not I would have a peaceful day.

I chose to come into an understanding with God. He would have the final say over my life, and that life did not include fear and anxiety. It would encompass peace, freedom, confidence, faith, hope, and grit. I was not going to lie down and accept crippling fear anymore. My lips would only speak the truth of His word and His desires for me.

We can all do this. Every single one of us has the ability to speak truth to ourselves. We need to be so careful with what we are vocalizing to our hearts and minds. Because we will believe what we say to ourselves. You are worthy of every positive, powerful, loving, kind, forgiving, and encouraging word that you speak to others. Those affirmations are not just for them!

Friends, we have one life. One! What are you saying to yourself? What lies are you believing? What words are you repeating in your mind over and over that are keeping you from what God has created you to be? Stop speaking the enemy's language to your heart. Pay attention to what you are feeding your mind with. What are you reading and listening to? Who are you hanging out with? The verse that tells us bad company corrupts good morals (1 Corinthians 15:33) is not just for our youth; it is most definitely for adults too.

Who do you want to become? Do you want to be strong? Then stop speaking weakness over your life. Do you want to be fearless? Then stop speaking fear into your heart. Do you want to be valued? Then stop degrading yourself and start speaking God's love for you! Do you want to be courageous? Then stop repeating the what-ifs and move forward. Do you want to be brave? Then do not let doubt into your spirit. Do you want to be unstoppable? Then let God have His way in your life and let Him fight for you. Do you want to stop believing lies about yourself? Then stop saying them!

Utter only truth to your heart even if you don't believe it at first. Whisper them; shout them if you have to but just get the truth inside of you so much that God's purpose is all you see. God is so willing and able to send you into the direction He created for you, but you have to want it. Are you okay with feeling less than what you were made for or do you want to feel intentional, valuable, and hopeful? You will only be what you tell yourself you are. You will only go as far as you say you will go. You will only do the things you say you will do. You will only fight for what you say you will fight for. So stop and ask: What am I telling myself?

Make It Happen

1. *Pray*: This seems like a no-brainer, but we need to stop, be still, and ask God to reveal the lies we are believing about ourselves. If you have faith that He will show you, then be prepared for the answer because He will.

2. *Write it down*: Write down your dreams and who you want to be. Be specific. Nothing is too big!

3. *List the lies*: Now, write down the lies you are speaking to yourself that are keeping you from accomplishing those dreams and *stop* saying them. Make a promise to yourself that you will not say them anymore. Date it and keep it as reminder of when you made this decision.

4. *Speak truth*: Get into God's Word and speak His love, grace, mercy, and truth over yourself. If you don't know where to begin, get the Bible app or go to the back of your Bible in your concordance and search for verses that speak life. Then, write them down and put them in your heart: memorizing them.

5. *Tell Satan to leave*: Yes, I just told you to talk to Satan. He is a very real entity. He can hear just like we can, and he is very intelligent. But guess what? If you have Jesus Christ living inside of you, his power is limited. So tell him to "kick rocks" as my husband would say. Tell him that you are not listening to him anymore and are not letting him have a say in your life. Say it out loud! One of the greatest deceptions that the enemy wants us to believe is that he is harmless. "Therefore, submit to God. Resist the devil and he will flee from you" (James 4:7, NKJV).

6. *Love yourself*: We will not take care of anything that we don't feel has value or is lovable. Ask God to help you value yourself, and then, you will learn to speak kindly to your heart. You are worth it, not because I say so, but because God says so. Live the life He wants for you!

CHAPTER 7

Lying

"Who broke my eraser?" My friend Lori was so upset after looking at her new pencil with an eraser that had been destroyed. It had her favorite dog, a Scottish Terrier, on it, and she was not happy that someone had ruined it.

She had invited me along with another little girl over to play for the day. I had broken the eraser but was afraid to tell her that I had been the one that did it. And I didn't really care for the other little girl that was there, so I blamed it on her. Lori was so angry at this little girl, and I was okay with the fact that I wasn't the one getting in trouble.

This incident is one of my very first memories of lying. Looking back now, I feel so horrible for that poor little girl. She hadn't done anything wrong and was only the victim of a jealous little girl who couldn't own up to her mistake. Of course, I had lied before this incident, but this one is the first clearest memory I have of purposely not telling the truth.

We all have lied. We did it as children and again as adults. We categorize lies into little white lies and huge lies. We justify them, feel guilty for speaking them, or do not care if we tell them. We lie to strangers, our children, spouses, friends, parents, coworkers and bosses, social media followers, and ourselves.

To not lie is usually one of the first lessons we teach our children when they can actually start communicating verbally to us. Lying is ugly and a character flaw that strongly marks a person once caught in a lie. It is very hard to come back from and to gain trust again in this area. It adversely affects every area of relationships and causes deep hurt, betrayal, and pain; making it so difficult to have close bonds with those who do lie to us.

Some of our lies have been hidden, and no one may ever find out, but some of our hardest, most destructive moments in our lives have started with what we would call big lies. Are certain lies worse than others? We like to call the less serious lies little white lies. Lying is lying no matter which way we look at it, but it is the size of the carnage left behind that usually has us rating the lie itself.

Some lies don't have serious consequences that we can see, so we own up to them and no one seems to have been hurt by them. But then there are the lies that can dismantle and end relationships. Then ones that render everyone involved with broken hearts. Lying is extremely destructive. Proverbs 11:3 (NIV) clearly points out this fact when it says, "The integrity of the upright guides them, but the unfaithful are destroyed by their duplicity."

Sadly enough, lying can become an extremely damaging habit; making a liar's words almost irrelevant. No one likes to listen to a liar and will end up not believing anything they say even when they are speaking the truth. Chronic lying is so destructive. It is Satan's language. The Bible says that he is the father of lies.

In John 8:44 (NIV), Jesus is speaking to the religious leaders of His time. He told them, "When he (the devil) lies, he speaks his native language, for he is a liar and the father of lies." I don't know about you, but I do not want to speak Satan's native language or be anything like him. There is no truth in the devil. He is a liar. Is that how we want to be thought of—a liar? I don't think anyone wants to be called a liar, but if you don't seek the truth or to speak it, you will fall into speaking lies.

In Proverbs 23:23 (NIRV), it says, "Buy the truth. Don't sell it. Get wisdom, training, and understanding." Truth is valuable and is in the same category as wisdom, training, and understanding. If we have truth, we need to hang onto it. All of these traits are what we should be striving for. Our reputations derive from our actions and our speech.

To be known as a truthful person is such an honor: for people to trust what comes out of your mouth; to know they can count on your words is priceless. Lying destroys all of that; making the trust hard to get back again. Can you get it back after lying? Of course, but it takes work, determination, and striving for truth. Do what you say you are going to do. Be where you said you were going to go. Take what is only yours and stay on an honest path. Being truthful is a life-style and a decision that only you can make. If we choose to not be honest, the consequences are painful and sometimes hard to handle.

Why do we lie? I believe there are two major reasons why people choose lies over truths: fear and selfishness. We are afraid of getting caught. We are scared of what others will think of us. We are fearful of facing our situation or trial. We really want something for ourselves and will do whatever it takes to get it. We care too much of another's approval and say or do what we need to gain it.

The scary thing is if we lie enough, our consciences become hardened to lying to where we don't feel guilty for not being honest. If we never feel guilty for lying, then how will we stop it? Lying is the enemy's number one tool; he uses it to get us far away from our God as possible. If he can get us to lie or believe a lie, then he will strategically use our lies to destroy our relationships, minds, and futures. He has a plan for all us, but we do not have to follow that plan. Deception is one of his devices to ruin everything we value, and that wreckage will always start with a lie.

Our words can be defined in so many ways. They tell people who we are and where we are going. They tell our listeners what is important to us and the condition of our hearts. Lying words say so much about us. They are telling the story of one of the most crucial aspects of our being: our character. So when we say untruths, no matter how sophisticated or calm, they scream "liar." They tell our hearers that we cannot be trusted, believed, or be a safe place for their words. Because if we throw around our words carelessly then what guarantees that we would treat theirs any better?

The lies that stem from fear are almost always the lies we start telling in our childhood. We didn't want our parents knowing what we did, so we lied to them. Sometimes, they found out right away, and other times, they found out later, but that was a chance we were willing to take. No little kid likes getting into trouble or grounded.

Now, I understand that some of you reading this had consequences that were unhealthy and dangerous forms of punishment from your parents, and no one would fault you for trying to be safe. That type of fear alone should have never been there to begin with. The type of getting in trouble that I am talking about is grounding, taking away our prized possessions for a time, time outs, for some of us spankings—just good old discipline. No one likes getting reprimanded by our parents, so as children we all tried to avoid it. Lying always seemed like the quickest and easiest way to avoid any kind of punishment.

My second oldest son went through a bad pattern of lying when he was about five. He lied about everything even if there would have been zero punishment for his actions. I didn't get it. Why was he telling me lies constantly? It got to the point that I could not believe him anymore. I became really worried that this would become a bad pattern in his life, so I tried to scare him into telling the truth by reciting the story of the little boy who cried wolf. Most of us know it.

I explained to my son that there was a little boy who took care of sheep and was always saying there was a wolf coming when there wasn't. So eventually everyone stopped believing him. Then one day, when an actual wolf really was coming towards him and his sheep, his cries fell on deaf ears because he had lied too many times.

The ending that I told my son was that the little boy was eaten because no one came to help him. When I had repeated to my mom what I had told my son, she looked at me and reminded me that the story ended in a sheep getting eaten, not the kid himself. Oh well. Hopefully I had put some fear into him to stop lying. I never said my parenting was perfect. We all do our best and do what needs to be done sometimes. Did he stop lying? No, he didn't. But he did not like the fact that his words would not be believed.

If you were the type of child that did not lie because you hated the guilt that came along with it, then I seriously applaud you. Integrity can be gutsy. Unfortunately, that was not me. I was raised in a good, moral, Christian home. I was taught very early, like most of us, that lying was extremely wrong and that the truth was always best.

I did not want to lie. I wanted my parents to trust me and to do the right thing, but sometimes my flesh would win, and I would listen to my mouth say things that I knew were not true. I didn't want to upset my parents or hear the word that every teenager hates more than anything: "No."

I wanted to do what I wanted and had no concept of what bad things could happen if I stepped outside of my mom and dad's safe boundaries they had set up for me. I knew more than them, remember? They were old and out of touch with the hip culture I was living in. I wanted to be where all of my friends were, so if that meant saying I was at a friend's house, so I could go to that orchard party (for those of us who grew up in farming and agricultural areas), then I would tell the lie.

I wanted to have fun, and my parents wanted me to not have fun, or so I believed, so lying seemed like the best way to get what I wanted. Selfishness drove me to not tell the truth. I was willing to get what I wanted and go where I wanted; sacrificing truth and my character to get there.

What about as adults? I mean, we should be getting better at building our character as we age, but we are most definitely not perfect. What do we lie about as we get older? Is lying still something that you struggle with? Why do we do it when we know that deep down it is destructive? Or do we realize how damaging it really is, not only to ourselves, but those around us?

The deadliest deception that Satan tells about the distortion of truth is that it cannot hurt anyone even us. He is so deceptive that he even lies about lies! I had a friend once tell me that what we have done and lied about will be brought to light whether it is a day, a week, a month, a year, five years, or thirty years, it will come out.

That consequence alone should be enough for us to have integrity in everything. And even though the repercussions are immediate, sometimes they are not felt or seen by the one telling the lie for a while. This very thing becomes the reason why people keep lying: they haven't got caught yet! They can keep going because they think no one will know!

Then there is the lie that has to be told to keep up the first lie. This is where it gets sticky. We tell a lie, but then that lie leads to more lies, so that the first lie can still be believed. Then another lie needs to be added; making it a web of lies that we can't even keep track of. If we had just told the truth to begin with, then we wouldn't ever have to be in those types of messes!

We really don't want our friends knowing that we didn't get that great job we just knew we were a shoe in for, so we told them that we got it. Now, we would need to lie about the times we went to and got off of work, lie around our plans and where we were, or just lie about the real reason we didn't get the job. We forgot to make that appointment, didn't really want to go to that party, were afraid we would pass out at that exercise class everyone is attending, so we come up with a lie that won't make us look bad in their eyes.

We don't want to look weak or unorganized to our friends that seem to "have it together." Maybe it's just the fact that we are insecure about our likes and dislikes, unable to voice them for fear of rejection. Or it could be that we know deep down we are flaky and can't seem to get honest with that part of ourselves, so we lie and act like we are on board with whatever it is we are asked to do. Sometimes we just need to learn to say no.

To some of you reading this right now, that word scares you. Not being able to say no can cause a lot of gigantic lies. There are actually whole books dedicated to that topic. If you hate or have a hard time saying no, then I would suggest that after you finish this book, you go out and get one on that. Our friends and family would have so much more respect for us if we actually told the truth.

What if we said, "You know I just can't commit to that because I probably won't go," or "That's not something I want to spend time doing right now but thanks for thinking of me." However, you choose to answer, do it with truth, and it will be so much easier to manage, and even if there is disappointment on the receiving end, they will respect you for your honest words.

Let's discuss how much I hate running. There is nothing in me that says, "Wow, that looks like fun!" when I drive pass a runner. I love to exercise though. I love HIIT training, TRX, Barre classes, yoga, Pilates, fast walking, lifting weights: you know, everything except running.

I have a beautiful friend named Kelly. She loves to run, and she is really good at it. She was always asking me to run, and I even agreed to running a 5k with her one time. (I don't even know who that woman was.) I did not want to run that 5k. The thought of it gave me anxiety, so I finally had to just tell her that I would more than likely never run with her so to stop asking me.

She laughed but understood. If I had kept on making plans to run with her, which I did a few times and am obviously still alive to tell the story, then I would have been constantly lying to her and myself. I am so confident in the fact that I am not a runner nor do I ever want to be. The end.

Let's talk about the famous lie: the truth will hurt their feelings. Does truth hurt? A lot of times it does. That's life. Is it fun being the bearer of "bad news"? Absolutely not. But hiding truth is equal to lying. Now, I understand that there are things we should keep to ourselves. We do not need to voice our opinions on our friend's choice of outfit, parenting decisions, or their house décor. We are not the end-all of knowledge, people.

The truth I am speaking of is the facts we know that have a considerable effect on the person. When we choose to tell these things to others, we will always run the risk of their reaction. Will they "shoot the messenger," or will they be grateful that someone decided to not hide the truth anymore? And, more importantly, we need to check the motive for our "why" in the revealing of those truths.

I have a great friend that has a son the same age as my younger two boys. Ever since our boys became friends, we made a pact: if our kids ever did anything wrong and the other mom found out first, we had to tell each other. We both had our share of "telling" things to each other, but we never got upset at the one exposing the misbehaving of our kids.

We had the other mom and son's best interest at heart. Our motives were pure, and we cared for each other and our kids. Did it hurt sometimes to hear what our kids had said or had done? Of course, but knowing was so much better than it being hidden. Raising four boys, I have obviously come into contact with a lot of moms and have been caught up in gossip.

The one phrase that I hated the most was when after all of the hearsays had been said, usually the one voicing the rumors would say, "Well, it's really none of my business." And she would be correct: it was none of her business. But we all feel brave in talking about the lies or truths being spread like wildfire amongst our communities and schools but never find the courage to actually tell the mom or wife or friend what we know.

Here's a little advice that we have all heard and need to start living out: if you wouldn't say it to their face, then don't say it at all. Telling the truth to people, especially our closest friends and family, may sting at first, but in the end, they will be grateful that we did the hard thing. Like I said earlier, integrity is gutsy. It takes some fearlessness sometimes to say tough things. But the care you have for your hearer is what should drive you for them to know.

I have had to reveal some of the most painful truths to close friends and family. I have had horrible truths reported to me. It's not fun. But we will all be more honored in the end and trusted when we can speak with certainty and accuracy. When others know that our words are always factual and legitimate, they can trust us with their words, their hurts, and their joy.

I know that sometimes telling the truth is hard, and at that moment in time, the lie seems so much easier. And, sometimes, the lie can be easier, but in the long-run, the truth will always win out as the best way. Colossians 3:9 says, "Do not lie to each other, since you have taken off your old self with its practices." When we accept Christ and are "new," we are not supposed to look the same. That means that we should act different, think different, and speak differently than we did before we knew Him.

If lying is Satan's language, then the truth is God's. Jesus told his disciples in John 14:6, "I am the way, the truth, and the life. No one comes to the Father except through me." Jesus is the truth. When we speak, our words tell others who we follow. Are we following Jesus who is truth or Satan whose native language is lying?

I know some of you are probably thinking to yourself, "Oh, Chessa, aren't you taking this a little far?" But am I? Why would we not take God's Word seriously? Why would we not try and follow Christ's way and words when He is the very one who created us and knows us better than anyone ever could. He knows what is best and what will harm us in the end. Like Proverbs 16:25 reads, "There is a way that appears to be right, but in the end it leads to death." There are lies that seem right at the time, but in the end they can lead to death. Lies are not life-giving words, friends, they are words of death.

I want to talk about God's character here. Did you know that it is actually impossible for our Creator to lie? Impossible. Absurd. Preposterous. Inconceivable. It ain't never gonna happen. (Like my good grammar there?) It is completely against the core of who He is.

In 1 Samuel 15:29, it says, "He who is the Glory of Israel does not lie or change his mind; for he is not a human being, that he should change his mind." I love this. I love how God shows us that He does not make mistakes like we do. He will not fail. He can be trusted. Humans will lie, but God does not. He is not like us. He existed before us and is perfect in every way.

To know this means that we can rely on Him. When speaking to Isaiah, the prophet, in chapter fifty-five verse nine, He told him, "As the heavens are higher than the earth, so are my ways higher than your ways and my thoughts than your thoughts." God's ways are infinitely beyond ours, so when He expresses His heart about lying and truth, we better take notice.

God is the perfect parent. He does not have to guess what is best for us because He knows already. God did not have to learn truth because He is the truth. He didn't have to find His way because He is the Way. God did not set boundaries for us to keep us from having fun like our teenage selves so badly wanted to think about our parents. All of God's laws and rules were set for our safety and to give us long and peaceful lives as much as possible while on this earth.

Just like how we keep our children from touching the hot stove or running out in the street, God does not want us lying to others or ourselves. We know the dangers of our kids breaking these rules in the same way that God knows the dangers and consequences of us breaking His. Don't misunderstand me here. I know that we have grace, mercy, and forgiveness, but we also need to have accountability, responsibility, and obedience. Just because we have grace does not mean we will not have consequences.

I love my children with all of my heart, but that is not going to keep them from getting second- or third-degree burns after touching the stove. I have unconditional forgiveness for my boys, but that is not going to keep their bones from being broken by a moving vehicle. God's love is not what's at stake here when we disobey Him, but the harmful results of our poor choices.

King David knew a thing or two about the ramifications of disobedience. He lived through the heartache and pain that came from his deception and lying. People had died because of his living outside of God's safe boundaries for him—even his own son. He penned these words in Psalm 119:45, "I will walk in freedom, for I have devoted myself to your commandments." He knew the destruction from speaking lies, but he also knew the freedom from following what God had asked him to.

David had touched the stove, ran out in the street and had the scars to prove it. There is no freedom in lying but only enslavement. Here I go again, overreacting to little white lies. What's the big deal? No one will get hurt. Those right there are the very lies that Satan will get you to believe about lies. Satan lies about lies! That is how tricky and underhanded he is. He knows the more lies we tell, the easier they will be to repeat.

In 1 Timothy 4:2, Paul says, "Such teachings come through hypocritical liars, whose consciences have been seared as with a hot iron." These people's consciences were numb and calloused. Lying was easy for them. Their seared consciences had no feeling towards what God wanted for them. This is what sin can do to us. If we are not careful to listen to our God, paying attention to what His best is for us, we will fall into practicing stuff that hardens and disables our ability to choose the next right thing.

Lying can become that one thing that is easy to do. This is not where you want to go nor who you want to be. But, just like our kids think they know better than us and are somehow immune to the repercussions of their choices, we can be the same way when it comes to obeying our Father.

Who are you going to trust in this area: Satan who only knows how to speak lies or your Creator who is only able to speak truth? Speaking the truth will not always be easy, but it is necessary for good relationships and peace, not only with others but with ourselves. We always have a choice on whether or not to tell a fib or to speak honesty. Integrity is always the best choice no matter how hard. The timing needs to be chosen in wisdom and spoken in love, of course.

It may be hard, and your hearer may not like what you are saying, but believe me, you will feel so much better about yourself in the long run. And, if the person hearing your truth is wise, they will appreciate it and respect you in the future; if not right then.

I have been the one no one believed because of too many lies; the one letting little white lies slip out for fear of what others would think; the bearer of bad news; and the one who heard hard-to-handle truths that almost stopped my heart. I have been on all sides of lying and truth. But one thing I have learned is that the truth will always win out. No matter what.

Make It Happen

1. *Honestly evaluate your integrity level: How honest are you?*
   On a scale from 1 to 10, 1 being "I strive for the truth no matter what" to 10 being, "I don't care if I lie as long as I come out looking okay," where are you? A lie is a lie, but over time lying can numb us to caring at all about whether we lie or not. Are you at the numbing phase of lying? These are serious questions to ask yourself. If you really want the

truth, ask someone close to you like a spouse or best friend and see what they have to say.

2. *Pray and ask God what your motive for lying is*: We all have lied or still lie, and God knows about every single, so why not ask Him to help you understand where they are coming from. The answer will help you to better fight the urge to skip the truth.

3. *Come clean*: By far the hardest one of all. If you have lies still hanging out, and you are the only one who knows it is a lie, then you need to come clean. Be honest with those you've hurt. Pray for guidance and wisdom in this area and how you need to go about doing this, but you will feel better for it.

4. *Tell the truth*! If you are used to lying, this will be hard. You have set a pattern of defaulting to dishonesty. Purposefully tell yourself that you will tell the truth. Write it down on a sticky note on your bathroom mirror if you have to. "*Be honest!*" Embed it into your heart and mind. Look up verses about honesty and lying. Read them daily if you have to. Ask God to help you in this area. He wants you to speak truthfully, so He will always be on your side in this!

"The path of honest people takes them away from evil. Those who guard their ways guard their lives" (Proverbs 16:17, NIRV).

CHAPTER 8

Worship and Praise

Shout for joy to the Lord, all the earth. Worship the Lord with gladness; come before him with joyful songs. Know that the Lord is God. It is He who made us, and we are his; we are his people, the sheep of his pasture. Enter his gates with thanksgiving and his courts with praise; give thanks to him and praise his name. For the Lord is good and his love endures forever; his faithfulness continues through all generations. (Psalm 100:1–5, NIV)

The words "worship" and "praise" are almost always linked to church services on Sunday mornings. We usually relate them to singing songs to and about our God. As Christians, we are taught the importance of worship, and we see it all throughout the Bible.

But how important are praise and worship, really? What part do they play in our lives, and how should we view words of praise and worship? Are they only meant for Sunday mornings during the twenty minutes or so of carved out time by our churches, or should we be spending more time in addition to that?

It seems like in today's American churches, our view of worship has become more of a style we prefer rather than what worship is actually for and what it does to our relationship with God and to us physically. Worshipping God is so powerful. It can be the door that opens up communication with our Father and the means by which we can hear him.

Worship is so vitally important that even beings in Heaven are constantly praising him day and night. "Each of the four living creatures had six wings and was covered with eyes all around, even under its wings. Day and night they never stop saying, 'Holy, holy, holy is the Lord God Almighty, who was, and is, and is to come'" (Revelation 4:8, NIV). This worship never stops. Ever. Think about that.

To express who God is, what He has done, what He will do, and what He means to us is our worship to Him. Worship means a reverent honor and homage paid to God or a sacred personage or to any object regarded as sacred; adoring reverence or regard. Praise means the act of expressing approval or admiration; commendation, laudation; the offering of grateful homage in words or song as an act of worship.

When we worship God, we admire Him and offer Him our gratefulness and approval. And, just to let you in on something, God doesn't lack any of these things. He doesn't need us or our worship to be anything. God is God by Himself, perfectly perfect, not in want of anything. The beautiful nature of this fact is that in God not needing us; his desire to have a relationship with us means that he chooses us. And, in return, He wants us to choose Him.

When we think about the love and relationship that we have with our children, we want them to love us because they want to, not because they have to or are forced to. The choice to love makes it rarer and exclusive if we know the person has preferred us. God wants us to love Him because of who He is. We are not robots being forced into a relationship with Him; we choose to love Him.

How do we learn to love someone? All relationships start with an introduction which then leads into learning about the other person. As we grow in these relationships, we begin to learn more and more of that person. Communication is key, otherwise, how would we be able to discover their feelings, likes, dislikes, personality traits.

All of these aspects are crucial not only to our human connections but also in how we associate with God.

He is a Person. He has likes and dislikes, personality traits and feelings. As with any friendship, we must talk to the other person. Prayer is vital to us growing closer to God. Reading about who He is and how He thinks of us in His word is paramount to how we will relate to Him. But the thing that stands out in our relationship with God is His sovereignty, power, and omniscience. He knows us better than we know ourselves. He knows what we need to have a great and fulfilling life with Him. And one of the most critical and necessary pieces of that satisfying life is to worship Him.

Words of worship and praise have not only a spiritual and mental effect on us but also a physical effect as well. In an article on joydigitalmag.com, Dr. Caroline Leaf, a cognitive neuroscientist and follower of Christ, stated the amazing and positive links between worshipping God and our health.

Without getting super medical and technical, she says in the article, "The emerging medical field of psychoneuroimmunology (the study of the effects of psychological factors on the immune system) is recognizing the central role of worship in the prevention, amelioration (make or become better), and cure of disease. Corporate worship has been shown to have health benefits. Amazingly, it has been found that as people sing together in worship to God, as in a choir for instance, as well as the beneficial effects of the heart, their heartbeats actually synchronize. In other words, their hearts beat as one." (The Effect of Worship on the Brain and General Health by Dr. Caroline Leaf found in "Joy! Digital," joydigitalmag.com)

Our response to who God is through worship and praise physically improves and contributes to our health! That is amazing! We were designed and created to worship Him. Our body's physiological response to worshipping our Creator reveals this fact. Words of praise to Him leave us better than we were before we started. Can you imagine what a life and attitude of worship would do to us, improve in our everyday lives, and responses to life's issues and problems?

What if instead of complaining or defaulting straight to our negative assumptions, we chose to praise and worship the Maker of

Heaven and Earth, the One who is in control of everything? The "created" exalting and praising their Creator sparks something in us. It makes a way for our betterment and healing. It creates space for an encounter with God.

Not only does our worship enhance our health, but it also affects beings and circumstances that we cannot see. If we spend enough time in the Bible, we will quickly see that there is a part of this world that is not physical. In fact, the spiritual realm is just as real as the one we are in right now. There are spiritual beings who are for us, and there are some who are against us. Both parties have the ability to see and hear.

Satan can hear what we say. He is wonderful at taking our negative words and using them as fuel against us. But worship and praise are words he cannot use. In fact, while we are speaking or singing words to our God, those same words are fighting against those who are trying to fight against us.

Worship is darkness-shattering. It is literally a weapon of war. When we worship with our mouths, we are declaring the truths of who God is and what He is able to do. We are announcing the greatness, mercy, grace, and everlasting love of our Creator. The amazing thing about worship is that when we are talking to Him and singing about Him, He begins to speak to us. He reveals His will and heart to us in those moments that we focus our minds and thoughts on Him.

It is so easy to miss phrases and words when we are talking to one person while texting another. We think we are hearing them both, but in reality we cannot fully engage or pay attention the way we can when we are speaking to one person at a time. It's the same with God. When we worship and our attention is fully on Him, He opens our spiritual eyes and ears to see and hear only what He can show us. The lines of communication seem to be a little clearer when we are praising Him. Our spiritual ears perk up when we desire to know what God has to say.

A great example of the power of praise and worship is found in Acts 16:16–34 (NIV). Again, if you don't know this story, stop now, grab your Bible or get on your Bible app, and read it! The Reader's Digest version is this: Paul and Silas did something that made the city officials mad, so they imprisoned them. But before they put the two apostles in jail, they were stripped and severely beaten with rods. Even though they were in immense pain, they sang and prayed to God. The scriptures say that the other prisoners heard them which meant the jailers that were in charge of the two men probably heard them too. Verse 26 says that, "Suddenly there was such a violent earthquake that the foundations of the prison were shaken. At once, all the prison doors flew open, and everyone's chains came loose."

Their praise and worship, even in the midst of their misery, showed their faith in God, and God moved on their behalf. The chains on their hands and feet were literally loosened. When the jailer saw what happened, he feared for his life. If any prisoners were lost on his watch, he would have been executed.

But when Paul and Silas saw the jailer about to take his life, they cried out to him and made sure he knew that none of them had left. When the jailer saw what God had done for them, he asked Paul and Silas what he needed to do to be saved, and the author, Luke, wrote that at that very hour, Paul baptized the jailer and his whole household.

There was power in Paul's and Silas's singing to God. That power was manifested in two ways: their chains were broken and the jailer saw evidence of God's power and believed in Jesus. Our praise and worship can break our spiritual chains just like it broke Paul's and Silas's physical chains. When others see our devotion and faith in God in our worship, it can grow their faith and encourage them to seek Him. One of the most moving things that I can witness is watching someone praise and worship God like no one is watching. The sincerity of verbally expressing love and gratefulness to our Savior is beautiful, not only to God but to those who witness it.

God is so deserving of all the praise we could ever give him even in our imperfection. We will never ever be able to sing enough praises, speak enough of his glory, or worship him the way his goodness and perfection demands. We are never going to be enough. That alone makes his love for us even that much more incredible which humbly commits us and calls us to worship him.

It's always easy to worship God when things are going the way we had planned, but when we have mountains to climb and problems to overcome, worshipping isn't always the first thing on our minds. We love to say how good God is when everyone is healthy and all of our needs and wants are being met. Our words of praise are effortless when we get that raise, that new car, or good doctor's report.

But what about when none of those happen? How does our worship fare when our children are sick or we or our spouses lose their jobs? What about when we lose our homes or just cannot seem to get ahead financially while it seems that everyone around us is? Life is not always going to be good or fair. Jesus said Himself, "In this world you will have trouble. But take heart! I have overcome the world" (John 16:33, NIV).

Hard and difficult situations are going to come our way. We can be sure of this. At some point in our lives, money will be scarce, jobs will be in danger, relationships will fail or be tested at the very least, loved ones will get sick and some will die. People that we trusted will betray us, and our hearts will get broken.

I will never forget one time helping out in my second oldest son's, Luke, class when he was in second grade. It was the last day of school, and the teacher had a fun party for all of the kids. It was a really fun day for all of them. At the end of the day the teacher stood up in front of the class and began directing questions to the children to see if they had remembered some important things she had taught them.

One of them was, "Kids, what did I tell you this year?" All of the boys and girls responded in perfect unison, "Life's not fair." At the time, I laughed and laughed at all of these sweet, precious seven-year-olds saying an age-old saying about a life that they had nearly started. I still smile about that day because it is funny, but it is so very true. Life isn't fair. It hardly is. None of us will get the end of our existence here on this earth unscathed or free from pain. Obstacles and complications are inevitable. We will have trouble in one form or another.

For some of us, our response to hard issues in our lives is to either try and fix it ourselves or run to another broken human to see if they have the answer we are looking for. A good listening ear is always helpful. God wants us to lean on and lift each other up. He created the church and community for this very reason. We do not have to live this life, good or bad, by ourselves.

But sometimes we default ourselves to go to people and forget to meet with our Father. He alone has the perfect answer. I believe it is in the waiting for an answer sometimes that causes us to run to others first. We can get an immediate response from a human talking to us and our ears receiving words.

God doesn't always work that way. The waiting is the hardest. We want an answer now, not tomorrow or a week from now. If we allow ourselves to wait for God's answers, it is usually in the waiting where we grow from our pain and become ready for the response. It's almost like God is preparing our hearts for what is to come. The wait does so much for us, much more than we could ever realize.

What does this have to do with worship? Everything. In our expectations of God's resolution to our problems, we usually forget that we play a part in the conversation. Of course, we need to listen to what He is going to tell us, but there is one important element that we seem to lose sight of and that is to worship.

Worshipping God while in anticipation is influential in how we wait. The worship itself is the anchor preparing us to hear from Him. If we focus on praising Him in the space between our request and His reply, the wait holds power. It grows our faith, our hope, and our expectation.

God always answers us in the perfect time with the perfect solution. If we truly believe this, then we will look forward to the reply. When we worship Him during the wait, we are affirming our devotion, focus, hearts, and belief in who He is and what He is capable of. The worship tells Him that we know He is able, loving, and always right. Praising Him creates a place in our hearts and minds that says, "No matter what the answer, I know it is God's very best for me."

Verbally expressing our love of God and description of who He is designs an acceptance of what will be. When we speak the attributes of God—about his goodness, power, love, faithfulness, omnipotence, grace, mercy, eternal existence and His plans for us—our love for Him increases, and we mature in the way we view Him.

To view God as a vending machine figure that gives us what we want if we give Him what He wants is an immature perspective to have. That's not how God works. Praising Him can sometimes be even more dynamic when we accept the possibility that we may not get what we want.

It also humbles us to know that we are not capable of what God is capable of. We cannot ultimately save ourselves or fix our situations. We need Him to do what we cannot, to go to places we do not have access to, and to see what we cannot see. Worshipping Him is our response that says we know He is in control, that He sees and understands us, and that no matter what happens He is still God and we are not. When our faith in Him is spoken, things begin to happen in us and the atmosphere around us—seen and unseen.

What do these words of praise look like? What words constitute as worship? The Bible is full of examples of worship and praise from believers who followed and loved the exact same God we worship today. The book of Psalms is the most popular book to go to for words of worship because King David was a psalmist and wrote many songs talking about God and who He is.

The King of Israel worshipped in pain, suffering, regret, joy, contentment, want, success, failure, love, and grief. The book of Psalms is an amazing picture of how God is always with us in our vast emotions. The common thread that we see when reading David's worship to God is David's faith in who God was and who David wasn't. No matter what season of life David found himself in He knew God was in control. Even when God wasn't showing up exactly the way or in the timing David would have liked, he still confirmed his faith and love for his heavenly Father.

The king's worship always reflected what he knew to be true of God. The Bible says that David was a man after God's own heart. Let that sink in for a minute. God was pleased with David. David's heart was in love with his Creator. Their relationship did not just happen by chance. I believe that one of the main reasons of this was found in David's undying love, devotion, and worship of God.

His faith and words came together to create beautiful worship that is an inspiration of most of the worship music we hear today.

"To you, Lord, I call; You are my Rock, do not turn a deaf ear to me. For if you remain silent, I will be like those who go down to the pit. 2 Hear my cry for mercy as I call to you for help, as I lift my hands toward your Most Holy Place" (Psalm 28:1–2).

In these verses, we can see that David is in desperate need for God to move in his life. He needs to hear from God. And, in the midst of his cries for help, he recognizes that God is his Rock and that the place God dwells is holy. This is praise in the middle of asking to be saved. David goes to God because He is the Rock and the One who is able to rescue the king.

I think one of my favorite aspects of David's Psalms is his honesty. He is not afraid to tell God to not be silent, to not leave him where he is, to not forget him, and to remember His faithfulness and promises to His children. Even though David knows that God is all-powerful and sovereign, he still allows his human feelings to come out to say, "Hey, God, I know what you can do, but this is really hard, and I don't know how much longer I can hold on. Are you even listening to me?"

It is in these prayers that David's worship stands out as the power source of getting God's attention. We see him just being real and voicing his feelings to God. It's the "but no matter what God, You are always good" posture that David reveals in his Psalms.

Pain is something we all will feel in our lifetimes: emotional pain, physical pain, spiritual pain. It is inevitable. People either respond in two ways: blame God or worship God. Blaming God for our pain and suffering can be the easy way out because God is the only one who has the power to remove our pain. By blaming Him, we can focus our anger, pain, and suffering towards Him.

Worshipping Him during the pain can be the hardest because we know He can remove it, and when He chooses not to, we do not understand why. We worship with no answers, no knowing, no end in sight. Choosing to worship says that we trust God and His timing; His love and all-knowing existence. Worshipping Him during difficult seasons does not mean we enjoy the pain or even that we understand why it is happening. It says to Him that we recognize His goodness no matter what happens. It says to others who our faith is in and where we place our lives.

Probably my all-time favorite Bible story is found in the book of Daniel, chapter 3. If you have never read this story, stop reading this and go grab your Bible. Now. Everyone needs to know this story.

Shadrach, Meshach, and Abednego stayed faithful no matter what pain was in front of them. They trusted God with their lives and never faltered in their belief that God was sovereign and always right and good even if that meant they would suffer. They were commanded to worship a false god, but when they disobeyed the King, their consequence meant burning alive in fire.

Their faith-filled answer to the King is what moves my heart closer to God even when His answers are not what I want. Daniel 3:16–18 says,

> Shadrach, Meshach, and Abednego replied, "O, Nebuchadnezzar, we do not need to defend ourselves before you. If we are thrown in to the blazing furnace, the God whom we serve is able to save us. He will rescue us from your power, Your Majesty. But even if he doesn't, we want to make it clear to you, Your Majesty, that we will never serve your gods or worship the gold statue you have set up."

The God whom we serve *is* able. But even if He doesn't… Even if He doesn't take this pain, suffering, hardship, illness, oppression away. Even if. What will you do? What will be or what has already been your response? Will you blame or worship? Will you praise him and his faithfulness and goodness even in your questioning, or will you accuse a loving and infinite God that he was wrong?

This is so important for us to grasp in our relationship with God. He is God, and we are not. He is perfect, and we are not even close. We need to know and embrace this fact. When life is good, God is good. When life is bad, God is still good. Sometimes we forget this. Even though we would love to get everything we want from Him, His goodness and perfection is the very reason why we go to Him in the first place. We wouldn't ask him for the right answer if we did not believe the answer would be right in the first place.

So if we understand that His answers are always true and correct, then we need to be able to welcome the outcomes we want right alongside the one's we do not. Worship is one of, if the not the single most important way, to use our words. Everything He created has the ability to worship him. And, after knowing him and what he did to save you and have a relationship with you, how can you not worship him?

Make it Happen

1. What is your default reaction when difficult circumstances arise in your life? Do you blame or worship? Or do you try and deal with it on your own? Prepare your heart to worship God the next time a situation comes up that is hard to handle. Set your mind to praise Him instead of blame or ignore Him. I guarantee that your heart and perspective will be different after the situation than when you entered it.

2. Truly focus on Him during corporate (church) worship and the words you are saying. Lift your hands, clap, close your eyes—anything that helps you be in a posture to close off what's around you and worship your Creator.

3. Be prepared to receive. God can speak to you any time He chooses. But there is something so special about the interaction that happens between us and God when we sing His praises and honor Him with our words. Listen for Him to speak to you as you worship.

4. How do you worship Him when you are not at a church gathering? Try downloading your favorite worship music, find a Christian radio station, write down your favorite verses that praise God or verbally express His amazing attri-

butes in prayer to Him. Do not wait until church service to praise God. Do it every day.

5. If you really want to dig deep, do a word study in the Bible on worship and praise. Look up all of the verses and stories in the New and Old Testaments about worshipping. It will grow and strengthen your faith! If you don't know where to start, begin with the book of Psalms.

CHAPTER 9

God's Words

Enough about our own words. Even though, I know that's what I wanted to talk to you all about in this book. But can I tell you that none of our words will ever mean anything past this life if we do not have our Creator's words in our hearts? There will never be anything more important or life-changing than the words of God Himself. I firmly believe that one of the top deficiencies in the body of Christ today is the lack of reading and knowing the Bible.

The western church has so many distractions and "more important" things to do with their days. We will fill up our schedules with everything from work to school, kids' sports, vacations, "me time", parties, Netflix, TV, even church activities—you name it, we are busy with it. None of these are bad in and of themselves, but where does God fit in? What do we have to limit to squeeze in time to listen to God and read His word? Why are we so afraid to sacrifice something we dearly love just so that we can read for twenty minutes and deepen our relationship with God?

Our mantra as Americans has become, "I am so busy!" It has almost become a badge of honor: something to be proud of. But this busyness that we can't seem to get control of has pushed the Bible aside. Reading it has not become one of the "must haves" of our days. We'd rather read books written by humans and lean on their wisdom instead of reading words from the one who designed us and the world we live in.

I say this knowing that you have my book and words in your hands! People have amazing and extremely helpful things to say. I have received some insanely, wonderful knowledge from humans that I admire and love. I love to read books on all kinds of topics, but I know that those cannot be the only source that I receive knowledge from on how to live my life and look at the world. While other books can help us better our lives and perspectives, they should not become our default or main origin of insight. Who better to go to than the One who made it all?

The deceptive part of these distractions is that the distractions are not always bad things. It is not bad to spend time with family or go to our kids' games, volunteer for our church functions, watch a movie, read a book, go to work or school. Those are all good and fun things! Life is full of fun and not so fun events; things that must happen and things that we use to fill time.

In all of our busyness, we have forgotten to make time for the most important person we will ever know. I am always encouraging friends and family to go straight to the Word. In doing so, I have heard every excuse in the book of why it can't be done. We all have the same twenty-four hours in a day, and we are in control of how we spend that time. If our priorities do not include time in prayer and the Bible, we will suffer from it physically and spiritually.

The Bible is the only book that has ever existed that is alive. Yes, like actual living, breathing, moving, searching, and active. Hebrews 4:12 (NIV) says, "For the word of God is alive and active. Sharper than any two-edged sword, it penetrates even to dividing soul and spirit, joints and marrow; it judges the thoughts and attitudes of the heart."

Because God's word is alive, it reveals those places in your heart that need to be better aligned with Him and His purposes. God can speak to us in any way He deems necessary, but the most common way He speaks to His creation is through the written word. We see in 1 Timothy 3:15–17 exactly what the Bible does. It says, "The Holy Scriptures, which are able to make you wise for salvation through faith in Christ Jesus. All Scripture is God-breathed and is useful for teaching, rebuking, correcting and training in righteousness, so that the servant of God may be thoroughly equipped for every good work."

Again, we see that it literally has the breath of God infused into it. And if God is alive, then His word is alive. When we go to His word for wisdom and answers, we get teaching, rebuking, correcting, and are trained in righteousness or right living. He gives us all of this, so that we would be ready for every good work. His Word makes us wise and shows us how to be saved through Jesus! It is literally the blueprint to eternal life with Him! It has the answer to our way back to God.

Every word of the Old and New Testaments were handpicked by our Father to help direct us and reveal His heart and plan for us. Every letter, word, sentence, story, lesson was intentionally placed by a loving Creator who wants us to know Him and His Son, Jesus. Nothing in all of God's Word was placed there by accident or without His approval.

If we were living in the 1380s, when only the Catholic priests and Jewish high priests had copies of God's Word and we didn't speak Latin, Greek, or Hebrew, then I think we could safely say that we didn't have easy access to it. That would be pretty difficult. There were copies on scrolls of God's Word, but you had to go to a synagogue or Catholic church to even hear a reading from it. But we do not live during that time.

A man by the name of John Wycliffe translated the first Bible into English during that time: making it accessible to everyone, not just the clergy of the church. Can you even imagine what it would have been like to see the Bible in English for the first time and to actually have access to it whenever you wished? Well, we can actually imagine this because we have access to the Bible every day now in our language.

American's today have an average of four Bibles per household. I have seventeen in my own house in five different translations in addition to a Hebrew/Greek Bible. There are around nine hundred translations of the English Bible in print today. We can choose any translation that we "like," or we can just use the Bible app on our mobile devices and read it digitally. We literally have 24/7 access to God's Word. No excuses.

Sometimes, I feel though that this easy access has made us apathetic to the Word. It's almost too easy to get to. The majority of US citizens do not know how privileged and blessed they really are. Unfortunately, the rest of the world does not have it this uncomplicated. There are still 1,600 languages in the world that still need a Bible translation, and some of those countries do not even allow Christianity as a religion.

The country of Maldives only has the book of Luke in their language, and it is illegal to bring a Bible there for personal use. People in the persecuted church are literally dying to read one, let alone have one of their own, and we, western Christians, are living our lives without it. The very book believers in the two-thirds of the world are being beaten, imprisoned, and killed for believing in or owning is the same book that collects dust on our bookshelves and coffee tables.

What if we craved the Bible the way our brothers and sisters in Christ in the persecuted church did? Would you be willing to be beaten, let alone die, to own a Bible? How about smuggling Bibles into other countries just so followers of Jesus could hold one in their own language, in their hands, for the first time? Why are they so desperate for the very book we cannot even fit in twenty minutes to read?

The answer to that will be different to everyone. But it is a question we need to address. It is no coincidence that the very book that can save us is the one we cannot seem to pick up or know what to do with. We have an enemy that would love nothing more than for us to put reading God's Word on our "I'll do that later" list. Maybe, this is the very thing that you struggle with, or maybe you love the Bible and are amen-ing everything I am saying. My desire is that every Christian would know and feel the value of spending time with God reading His very words. The benefits are greater than anything you or I could imagine.

The most important aspect of God's Word is the story of our redemption, reconciliation, and salvation through Jesus Christ.

Those are big words, I know. But they are vital to knowing what was done for you when Christ came to planet Earth. He accomplished the most single important, life-altering, world-changing, never before nor ever again event in the history of humankind. No question. And He did it for you.

So, what do those big words mean? Why are they so important? Redemption is the act of being saved. God redeemed us through Christ's death (Colossians 1:13–14). Reconciliation is to reunite, make peace, or resolve. Jesus's death reunited us to God the Father and made peace between us. (Romans 5:10, 2 Corinthians 5:17–18). Salvation is deliverance from harm, ruin, or loss. When Christ died, He made a way for us to be saved from eternal pain and separation from God (Romans 5:9, Romans 10:9).

The Bible is the means by which we know and understand what God did for us all through Jesus. It is His words that speak of the most beautiful and life-changing sacrifice ever made. James 1:21 (NIV) says, "Therefore, get rid of all moral filth and the evil which is so prevalent and humbly accept the word planted in you which can save you." The "word planted in you" is the Word of God! The power of knowing God, believing His words, and believing in the One he sent to us is our salvation.

Our relationship with God doesn't just stay at a standstill once we are saved. There is more. We still need the Word of God to infiltrate every aspect of our lives. If we are living beings, then we need a living book. We need something to speak to us in the here and now. We need a book that is timeless, and that's the Bible.

No matter how long ago the Bible was written, people are people. We all deal with the same heart issues. Adam and Eve were dealing with sin and kid issues long, long before cars and cell phones were invented. Sibling rivalry, jealousy, murder, adultery, lying, cheating—you name it. Whatever is being done now was in people's hearts then. King Solomon wrote in Ecclesiastes 1:9 (NIRV), "Everything that has ever been will come back again. Everything that has ever been done will be done again. Nothing is new on earth."

Humans have always had the same sin problems, same failings, same desires, same wandering hearts and minds. God knew this when He created us, so He gave us a book that would outlast our brokenness and actively speak to us as much today as He did the day He created mankind.

Since we are human and will fail and sin until we go on to be with God, we are in desperate need of instruction. James 1:22–25 says,

> Do not merely listen to the word, and so deceive yourselves. Do what it says. Anyone who listens to the word but does not do what it says is like someone who looks at his face in a mirror and, after looking at himself, goes away and immediately forget what he looks. But whoever looks like into the perfect law that gives freedom, and continues in it—not forgetting what they have heard, but doing it—they will be blessed in what they do.

Phew, lots of words in those verses! So, let's make it applicable and Cliff-note it.

What happens when you go look in a mirror and you see a big green leaf in your tooth? Well, if you care about personal hygiene and the person you might be kissing later, you will get it out! What if you see your mascara smudged under your eye? You wipe it. How about that red spaghetti stain on your new white shirt? (a) You try your hardest to get it out with water and maybe some hand soap *or* (b) You get that Tide pen out of your purse and use it.

Isn't that what mirrors are for? They show us our reflection. They let us know if something is out of place or needs to be fixed. And what good would the mirror be to us if we looked at that green leaf, smudged mascara, or spaghetti stain, did nothing about it and walked away?!? That wouldn't be very smart. Well, guess what? That is exactly the same effect the Bible has on us as we walk more and more with God and live in His will and purpose for us.

We read the Bible, and just like a mirror, we think, "Wow. I really need to implement that in my life," or "Uh-oh. I do that thing that God says will be destructive." The more time we spend in the Word, the more we see how much we need Him, how much better we are when we live out His principles and precepts, and how much He loves us broken, imperfect people. It is His Word that shows us the green leafs, smudged mascaras, and spaghetti stains on our souls.

He does not show us these things to shame us but to say, "Hey, come to me so I can clean that for you." He wants us to live our best lives. The Bible is literally a lifeline and handbook on how to live our most productive, joyful, peaceful, and strengthened years while on this earth. To read the Word, see what we need to change in our lives, then walk away, and ignore what we read is very dangerous. We need to pay attention to what God is telling us through His written word.

The power of God's words is something we can only grasp partially while we are still here, at home in our flesh. For those of us who do spend time regularly in the Bible, we begin to remember and memorize certain verses and stories. Then, when life throws a hard-ball at us, a friend or spouse betrays us, our kids go sideways, or we just have a rough day, the Holy Spirit reminds us of what we have put in our hearts from scripture, and it becomes power to us.

But how can it be a dynamic force in our lives if we do not know it? How can we see the effectiveness and strength of His word if we do not use it? Jeremiah 23:29 (NIV) says, "'Is not my word like fire,' declares the Lord, 'and like a hammer that breaks a rock into pieces?" His word can obliterate and destroy the lies and strongholds that try to tear us down. His word has the power to burn down the walls that close us off from freedom in Christ. His word is able to shatter what Satan has tried to build up in your heart and mind.

The amazing thing about fighting the enemy is that we do not need to use our words: we can use God's. God's words are enough to battle and war against a very real and present danger to our souls. I feel like I need to stay this again: you and I have an enemy. He is as real as this book or tablet that you are holding in your hand right now. He is as real as your husband, boss, coworker, friend, store clerk, or favorite actor. He is existing, living, and moving.

And he wants you broken, hopeless, defeated, bound, enslaved, and fear-ridden. He wants you so scared that you cannot move. He wants you so blinded in darkness that you stop hoping for light. He wants your mind so confused that you are unable to make a decision and move forward. He wants you stuck where you are, in the mud, at the lowest point of your life, and he is trying to hide the way out. I hope that sends a chill up your spine because it should.

But God. But God, my friends. He is the answer to anything the devil could ever conceive of doing to you. We have an answer, a light, a hope, a guide, and a healing to everything our enemy schemes for us. We have a way to fight back, a way to get our lives back, and in line with truth, a way to have spiritual oxygen breathed back into our souls. We have a weapon, and it is the Bible.

Are you seeing the scheming behind us desiring the word like we should? Satan will try anything to keep us from the very thing that will defeat him every single time. There is a reason why you are intimidated by the word, not willing to learn it, and distracted by so many things keeping you away from it. The enemy is lying to you to keep you from the power of our God's words. He doesn't want you reading, studying, or memorizing scripture. He wants you so busy with your life that you begin to believe and say out loud that you just do not have time. But to not have time for the Word of God is deadly to our relationship with Him.

We say we love Him, and we go to Him for help, but we don't have time to see what He has to say. That doesn't sound right, does it? What if we told everyone how much we loved our spouse, friend, or child, but we never listened to the very people we were claiming to love and know? What would it mean to tell people how important our family or friends were to us, but then turn around and say we don't have time for them? We all know that none of that makes sense.

If you want to get to know your Creator, then see what He has to say. If you want to defeat your enemy and start living your life in truth and power, then go to the source of that life and power! I would rather you read the Bible than any of my books ever again. That is how much I love it, and how vital I know it is.

I wish you could see my Bible right now. It is worn, torn, marked up, pages folded, and stained. It is used. I do not say that to make you feel bad or to make me look or feel better. I want to tell you this because I want you to be encouraged to grab yours, dust and all, or go buy one and start reading it.

My Bible had to start out brand new with crispy, clean pages and that wonderful new book smell. Which, by the way, I absolutely love. I smell new Bibles. Weird, I know. Start it today. Read one verse. Read two verses or read a chapter. Just get the most powerful words to ever grace humanity into your heart, mind, and soul. You will never regret it.

Make it Happen

1. *Start*: The number one response I get from people when I encourage them to get in the Word is, "I don't know where to start." And I totally get it! The Bible is a big book with big thoughts, ideas, stories, and unfamiliar concepts to some of us. I am here to tell you that it is okay! Start small. Begin in the book of John or Mark, Psalms or Proverbs, and literally read one verse today. Just one. Then each day add another verse, or if you are feeling hungry for more, read a whole chapter! Do not feel like you are not doing enough if you only get one verse in. You are reading it and are willing to begin, and that makes your Father so happy!

2. *Pray for the desire to read it*: God *wants* us to read His word. He desires for us to desire Him. He knows the power of the Bible and the changes it will make in you. Ask Him to give you the eagerness to get into His word. It is His will for us to know Him and know what the scripture says, so when we ask Him for this, He will answer it with a yes!

3. *Get into a Bible study*: If you are a part of a church, they more than likely have Bible studies set up. Join one. It will be a great place to learn and have accountability. You can also go online, and there are so many resources and websites to purchase your own individual study. Also if you have the Bible app, there are many daily devotionals that have scripture with them. If you don't have the Bible app, get it.

4. *Ask someone you trust*: We all more than likely know a Christian that we trust that has decent knowledge of scripture. Ask a friend, family member, or a pastor of your church to give you ideas on where to start, helps, and tricks on how to get going on spending time in the Bible.

5. *Carve out time*: Ouch. I know what you're thinking. "I'm so busy and don't have time to add one more thing!" Here's the cool thing about God. He knows everything, and I mean *everything*. So if you did step number two and said a prayer and meant it, the time issue will also be answered. Because God knows your schedule, and where you spend your time. Asking Him to give you a desire to read the word will open up ideas and initiative to make time for Him.

6. *Recruit a partner*: Do you have a friend that is struggling with wanting to read the Bible? Ask them to join you and keep each other accountable; coming up with a plan to get some verses in each day.

7. *Already in the word faithfully*? You love the Bible, are in a study, your Bible is marked up, and you have verses memorized already. That is *awesome*. Now you need to pray and ask God who he wants you to mentor in this area and encourage. Don't just keep the knowledge to yourself; share it with someone else! If you have great studying tips and strategies, share it!

CHAPTER 10

Legacy

I do not think we can talk about the importance of our words and not bring up legacy. The definition of legacy is "a gift of property, especially personal property, as money, by will; a bequest" or "anything handed down from the past, as from an ancestor or predecessor." When we "hand down" something to someone, we are giving them something that belonged to us, but is now going to be used for their use.

I am sure when it comes to material legacies, they are not always items we would choose ourselves. Some items we like, and others we have no idea what to do with them. Certain possessions that belonged to our grandparents or parents have special and sentimental value while others only meant something to them while they were living.

Both my husband and I were given Bibles that belonged to our grandfather and grandmother respectively. Those hold very special meaning and are sitting out in our living room as a reminder of our grandparent's legacies as believers. I have a rocking chair given to me by my mother-in-law, and it holds special meaning because it was the chair that she rocked my husband in as a baby. It sits in a corner of my bedroom, and is a reminder of the special relationship of my husband and his mother. She is still living but handed it down just the same.

You may be thinking right now of that special item: platter, bowl, table, picture, book, dress, watch, whatever it is that was handed down to you. It means something. It is special because it belonged to someone you loved and who held a very special place in your life. You may even have something that belonged to a distant relative a few generations before you whom you had never met but knew from stories of who they were and what they enjoyed.

When we talk about our past relatives, what is one of the things about them that we usually remember the most? What they did, and what they said. We have all heard or said ourselves, "My grandma used to always say…" Or our grandpas, aunts, uncles. There always seemed to be something that they would quote or a distinct instruction or word of wisdom or sometimes a not-so-nice word or phrase. We remember the most, among other things, their words. Our words are a legacy.

How many quotes do we read and see all over social media or in books? People are known by their words whether good or bad. How we speak to others, and what we talk about will follow us even after we are gone. The good news is that if your speech is not what you would like it to be and you're still breathing, you have the ability to change what you are vocalizing today—right now. Because even before we leave this life, your words will precede you.

We all have reputations now among our peers and others of how we convey our feelings. The legacy of our words is the lasting impression of how we used our words while were alive. Were they encouraging, helpful, loving, kind, gentle, wise, positive or degrading, spiteful, mean, vulgar, harsh, foolish, and negative? We all have words that have been spoken in each of these categories before and probably in the future, but what are the most common utterances that we use? What is the most common thread of our conversations?

Anytime we hear a person's name we are invoked with certain feelings that are usually indicative of past experiences or conversations with them. We almost always remember what they said and how we felt after being around them. Some people make us feel almost lighter after spending time with them. We love seeing them and having the opportunity to catch up on what's new in our lives.

These people are almost always encouraging, friendly, loving, and are good listeners. Their words help us and make us look forward to our next encounter with them. They more than likely are positive and uplifting and exude peace and balance. You pretty much know what to expect from them. These types of people make us feel better.

Then there are the others. The ones that we dread talking to. Their repertoire generally consists of, if not all, then ordinarily quite a few of these undesirable categories of words: negative, argumentative, gossip, rudeness, competition, selfishness, complaining, self-pity, doom, bragging, vulgarity, tactlessness, nosiness, condescending etc. I think you get it. Listening to these types of words drains us.

We feel heavier after hearing these people talk. We do not look forward to our next discussions with them. The instances that we try to avoid them become increasingly more. We all have times where we need to vent or get advice from someone on a lousy or sad situation. But there are people that seem to never have anything valuable to say. Nothing that would be constructive, productive, or for bettering their hearer. Their intention may or may not be to bring you down, but that is exactly what is accomplished. We can even be affected by way of becoming like these people if we are not careful. What we listen to always affects our hearts which in turn affects our words.

The words that we speak become what we are known for. With each syllable, we are creating our very own legacy. This is something that no one else can do for us. It is in our hands. We have the capacity to design and construct what words we will be known for. How we react to situations and handle problems with our words will be remembered long after we are gone. They also have the ability to affect others long after we are gone.

Words have the amazing ability to travel to any location or time period. We still have access to books that were written centuries ago. Statements and speeches given by American presidents and other world leaders are at our fingertips. The words these leaders have spoken have designed their legacy and have been handed down to millions upon millions of people. We can still gain knowledge from them.

How many of us have gone to conferences, trainings, or listened to messages and sermons preached on Sundays and have written down words that were given to us by the speaker? They framed a perception in our minds surrounding who the person was just by those words. Those phrases, quotes, and sayings were spoken and delivered from their hearts; giving us a glimpse of what they were thinking and what was important to them. All of these things wrapped up give us a peek into their legacy.

The older I get the more value I am placing on my words. My husband and I both have lost four grandparents between us in the last thirteen years has humbled my outlook on how I talk to my children and grandchildren. Each time a grandparent passed away, we would tell each other what that grandparent used to say to us. Their words stood out to us more than anything else. Their stories, wisdom, gentle guidance, and sometimes slip of a bad word were emblazoned in our minds.

I started to aspire for my children and grandchildren to one day remember the words I spoke as being a wonderful memory and not a hurtful one. Not every conversation I have with my boys is perfect and filled with grace and singing birds in the background like Snow White. I have said some not-so-nice things to my children, yelled when I shouldn't have yelled, and kept quiet when I should have spoken.

Not every single word that comes out of my mouth is wonderful and helpful. But I try to speak the best words possible to them. I don't always succeed, but I know what my intention is, and I strive to make sure what they are hearing will build up my legacy for great use. I want my instructions and loving guidance, even if it is not wanted at the time, to one day bring wisdom and benefit to them one day.

Laughter and joking is such a huge part of our family and is one of the character traits that I value in people, so I always try and make sure it plays a huge role in our home. I love to make my boys laugh, and I want part of my legacy to be of my humor and enjoyment of laughing.

I want them to remember me encouraging them to be their best even when they didn't believe they were capable. I want their memories of me to include strength in the face of trial and difficulty, faith when fear and doubt snuck its way into our lives, justice when

I saw something that was unfair, and grace when failure and embarrassment told them no one would accept them anymore.

I want my words to leave a legacy of forgiveness, determination, and love. I want the bad times and not-so-kind words to be drowned out by the pleasant and tender words. My desire is that my legacy of words would continue to empower and encourage even after I am gone. That my love for God and His Word through my conversations would be remembered by those I love is sobering to think about.

This book is full of my words and in the future will be read by people I will never have met but who will be impacted by them. To know that there will come a day when people will speak of me the way my husband and I spoke of our grandparents is surreal. Words of the past, phrases, and quotes memorized and brought to recollection when something reminds us of those who have passed on: that will one day be me. Every person reading this book will see a part of my legacy written in these very words.

What words spoken do you want to be remembered by? Will people describe you based on what you stood for or how you communicated to those around you? What phrases or instructions do you want imprinted on the hearts and minds of those closest to you? You have the power and ability to control what the legacy of your words will be. The wisdom of choosing our words carefully is within our reach. There so many things in life that we cannot control, but our words are one that we definitely can.

Positivity is contagious but so is negativity. What kind of atmosphere are you building around you with your words? You will be known by what you spoke while you were living. As long as you have breath in your lungs, you have the opportunity to create a legacy. Your very own legacy. And, whether we like it or not and whether a good or bad legacy, we will leave one.

Make it Happen

1. *Write down the words or types of words that you want people to remember you saying:* Writing things down can make them feel real. Put down on paper the words you want to

be said of you. Be honest and check to see if your words now line up with what you want your legacy to be.

2. *Fill your mind with good words*: What is in our hearts will come out in our speech. Pay attention to what you are filling your hearts and minds with. Are you allowing anything into your mind, or are you being careful and choosy to what and whom you listen to?

3. *Start today*! There's no time like the present! Start creating and changing your word-legacy *right now*! Send an encouraging text, email, or handwritten note to a friend or family member. Tell your child, husband, parent, coworker, or whoever is in within earshot that you love and/or appreciate them. We don't need to lie to give compliments because there is something good about almost everyone.

LAST WORDS

If I had a dime for every time I said, "Why did I say that?!?!" I would be a very rich woman. And, even after writing the first manuscript of this book I still have issues with every subject in each chapter. I still need the very words of this book as a reminder that I am human and need Jesus very badly to control my mouth. I wrote these words to hopefully show my readers how important our own words are and what an impact they have not only on others but ourselves. I also wrote it out of pure experience from a "talker extraordinaire". (If that's even a word).

There are so many things in life that we cannot control but our mouths are one of the things that we can. I pray that you take ownership of your thoughts, words and how you use them. My hope is that this book will remind you of the importance of how to handle your speech. I am most excited about changing your view of scripture and the very words of God himself. Be accountable for how much time you spend in the Bible. Spending time in God's Word will never return void. Trying to control the mouth without God's wisdom is like trying to turn on your lights when you haven't paid the electrical bill; the source isn't there.

After you are done reading this, mark it up, highlight in it, share it with a friend or buy some as presents for those that need a good mouth cleansing (if you received this as a gift, do not get mad at your friend and assume that is why she bought it for you). We can all use a good reminder more than once throughout our lives.

Most importantly, let God's Word be your guide and what you measure every thought, word and action against. We live in a world that teaches us to be our own truths and expects us to live in the culture of our day even if it means going against Jesus. Do not let your speech look so much like the world that no one knows whom you belong to. Speak truth when it is hard and keep silent when it is even harder. Glorify God with your words and not the status quo.

Never stop learning, growing and loving those around you. Never stop loving and spending time with Jesus. Until next time, speak well, friends.

Chessa is passionate about opening up God's Word for people and getting them excited about it. She loves people, laughing, talking, and chocolate. She and her husband, Justin, live in a small town in the central valley of California where they are living their best lives raising the last three of their four amazing boys and enjoying being first time grandparents to their granddaughter. When she is not writing, she is doing a lot of other really cool things that writers do.

CPSIA information can be obtained
at www.ICGtesting.com
Printed in the USA
LVHW020027310520
656910LV00006B/600